Mary Wilkins Freeman

Revised Edition

Twayne's United States Authors Series

David J. Nordloh, Editor

Indiana University at Bloomington

TUSAS 122

MARY WILKINS FREEMAN
(1852–1930)
From *Cosmopolitan,* March 1903.

Mary Wilkins Freeman

Revised Edition

By Perry D. Westbrook

State University of New York at Albany

Twayne Publishers
A Division of G.K. Hall & Co. • *Boston*

humca

Mary Wilkins Freeman, Revised Edition
Perry D. Westbrook

Copyright 1988 by G.K. Hall & Co.
All rights reserved.
Published by Twayne Publishers
A Division of G.K. Hall & Co.
70 Lincoln Street
Boston, Massachusetts 02111

Copyediting supervised by Barbara Sutton.
Book production by Janet Zietowski.
Book design by Barbara Anderson.

Typeset in 11 pt. Garamond
by Compset, Inc., Beverly, Massachusetts.

Printed on permanent/durable acid-free paper
and bound in the United States of America

Library of Congress Cataloging-in-Publication Data

Westbrook, Perry D.
  Mary Wilkins Freeman / by Perry D. Westbrook. — Rev. ed.
    p.   cm. — (Twayne's United States authors series ; TUSAS 122)
  Bibliography: p.
  Includes index.
  ISBN 0-8057-7523-4
  1. Freeman, Mary Eleanor Wilkins, 1852–1930—Criticism and
interpretation.   I. Title.   II. Series
PS1713.W4 1988
813'.4—dc19   88-11138
                                                                        CIP

In memory of my mother,
Madeleine D. Westbrook

Contents

About the Author

Perry D. Westbrook is professor emeritus of English at the State University of New York at Albany, where he was on the faculty from 1945 to 1983. Previously he had taught at the University of Kansas, the Georgia Institute of Technology, and the University of Maine. He received his A.B., M.A., and Ph.D. degrees from Columbia University. He wrote his doctoral dissertation, *Acres of Flint: Writers of Rural New England, 1870–1900* (published in 1951), under the supervision of Lionel Trilling, and thus began his lifelong interest in New England culture and literature. Westbrook has also written the following books on New England subjects: *Biography of an Island, The New England Town in Fact and Fiction,* and three in the Twayne United States Authors Series—*Mary Ellen Chase, Mary Wilkins Freeman,* and *William Bradford.* His other books are *John Burroughs* (also in the Twayne Series), *The Greatness of Man: An Essay on Dostoyevsky and Whitman,* and *Free Will and Determinism in American Literature.* He has also edited two anthologies of New England writings—*Seacoast and Upland* and (in collaboration with his wife, Arlen R. Westbook) *The Writing Women of New England.* He has held a Guggenheim fellowship, a Eugene Saxton fellowship, and a Fulbright lectureship in Kerala, India.

Preface

I first became interested in Mary Wilkins Freeman's writings about 1950 while working on a book (*Acres of Flint,* 1951; revised edition, 1981) dealing with New England "local colorists" of the period from the end of the Civil War to 1900. The governing idea of the book was that a group of authors, most of them women, had found in the then depressed, demoralized, and partly deserted New England countryside material for fiction and nonfiction of true literary merit and deep human significance. These authors included Sarah Orne Jewett, Rose Terry Cooke, Lucy Larcom, Celia Thaxter, Elizabeth Stuart Phelps, Alice Brown, Harriet Beecher Stowe, Roland Robinson, and, of course, Mary Wilkins Freeman. I emphasized about Freeman her analyses in the earlier stories and novels of the post-Puritan conscience and will in their almost pathological manifestations among the inhabitants of the run-out farms and the impoverished villages.

Fifteen years after researching *Acres of Flint* I wrote the book of which this volume is a revised edition. In the first edition I considered the entire body of Freeman's writing during close to fifty years of authorship, though I still kept the emphasis on works written before her marriage in 1902. A major focus was Freeman's treatment of the will and the conscience, but equal attention was given to the social and economic conditions of New England, not only in the rural areas but in the mill towns, as they affected the lives of Freeman's fictional characters. Other aspects of her work—for example, her literary experimentations and the qualities of her prose style—were discussed, as was her reputation as an author up to that time.

Mary Wilkins Freeman was a prolific and many-sided writer whose full significance, after years of neglect, is becoming more and more apparent. She has received growing recognition, particularly among academic critics, and she has been the sole subject, or a shared one, in a sizable number of Ph.D. dissertations. Articles on Freeman are steadily appearing in the scholarly journals, and reprints of her books and collections of her stories are now available. Recently, one of her tales, "A Mistaken Charity," was produced as a television drama. Finally, her extant letters—a boon to all who may write about her—have been edited by Brent L. Kendrick in a volume titled *The Infant Sphinx: Collected Letters of Mary E. Wilkins Freeman* (1985).

Freeman was, and remains, a perceptive recorder of the social and psychological effects of rural New England's decline upon the men and women who lived there. Her dissections of the latter-day Puritan will and conscience are detailed and convincing. But recent criticism has begun to perceive much more in her writings. For example, no one today would classify her as merely a "local colorist" or a "regionalist" in the narrow sense of those terms. Her characters are not just quaint Yankee rustics but real people struggling to cope with problems common to the human lot: poverty, loneliness, guilt, self-fulfillment, and self-esteem. The rural world in which so much of Freeman's fiction takes place was, for reasons to be discussed, very much a woman's world, but also one in which traditional male social, religious, and political dominance held full sway. Freeman's focus on the frustrations, struggles, and frequently successful coping of women so situated has been a concern of recent criticism, which has revealed a hitherto largely unnoticed area of significance in her work. In reassessing Freeman's writings, the following pages take this and other recent criticism into account.

The reader may note that in the title and text of this book I have dispensed with the initial E (for Eleanor) that Mary E. Wilkins Freeman always included in the name under which she wrote both before and after her marriage. In so doing I have been able slightly to differentiate this book from Edward Foster's fine biography *Mary E. Wilkins Freeman,* and I am also following a practice common among commentators on Freeman from Henry James to the present.

Perry D. Westbrook

State University of New York at Albany

Chronology

1852 Mary Ella (later changed to Eleanor) Wilkins born 31 October in Randolph, Massachusetts, to Warren Wilkins, carpenter, and Eleanor Lothrop Wilkins.

1859 Starts school. Her sister Anna is born.

1867 Moves with family to Brattleboro, Vermont. Enters high school.

1870 Graduates from high school. Enters Mount Holyoke Seminary.

1871 Leaves Mount Holyoke because of ill health. Takes courses at Glenwood Seminary, West Brattleboro.

1873 Meets Hanson Tyler, for whom she entertains romantic feelings throughout her life. Attempts, unsuccessfully, to teach at a girls' school. Her father's business fails, and he returns to carpentry.

1876 Anna Wilkins dies.

1880 Mother dies.

1881 *Wide Awake,* a magazine for children, accepts her ballad "The Beggar King." Places other poems in the same periodical and in *St. Nicholas.*

1882 Receives fifty dollars from the *Boston Daily Budget* for her first story for adults, "The Shadow Family."

1883 Father dies while on a construction job in Gainesville, Florida.

1884 *Harper's New Monthly* accepts her story "A Humble Romance." Returns to Randolph to live.

1885 Trip to New York and Brooklyn.

1887 Harper publishes *A Humble Romance and Other Stories.*

1891 *A New England Nun and Other Stories.*

1892 Meets her future husband, Dr. Charles Manning Freeman, in Metuchen, New Jersey.

1893 *Jane Field* and *Giles Corey, Yeoman: A Play.*

1894   *Pembroke.*

1895   *The People of Our Neighborhood.*

1896   *Madelon.*

1897   *Jerome, A Poor Man.* Suffers from poor health with nervous symptoms. Becomes engaged to Freeman.

1898   *Silence and Other Stories.*

1899   *The Jamesons.*

1900   *The Love of Parson Lord and Other Stories* and *The Heart's Highway.*

1901   *Understudies* and *The Portion of Labor.*

1902   Marries Freeman 1 January at Metuchen.

1903   *Six Trees* and *The Wind in the Rosebush and Other Stories of the Supernatural.*

1904   *The Givers.*

1905   *The Debtor.*

1906   *By the Light of the Soul* and *"Doc" Gordon.*

1907   *The Fair Lavinia and Others.*

1908   *The Shoulders of Atlas* wins *New York Herald*'s transatlantic novel-writing contest. Joins with Howells, Henry James, and others in writing the "cooperative novel" entitled *The Whole Family.*

1909   *The Winning Lady and Others.* Husband enters a sanatorium because of alcoholism.

1912   *The Yates Pride: A Romance* and *The Butterfly House.*

1914   *The Copy-Cat and Other Stories.*

1917   *An Alabaster Box.*

1918   *Edgewater People.*

1920   Husband committed to New Jersey State Hospital for the Insane at Trenton as a confirmed alcoholic.

1921   Husband escapes from hospital and temporarily resides at home.

1922   Legally separated from husband.

1923   Husband dies, having disinherited his wife. The will is later successfully contested.

1926   Receives from the American Academy of Letters the William Dean Howells Gold Medal for Fiction. Elected to membership in the National Institute of Arts and Letters.

1927   *The Best Stories of Mary E. Wilkins,* edited by Henry W. Lanier.

1930   Dies 13 March in Metuchen.

Chapter One

A Young Writer in
New England

Mary Wilkins Freeman is our most truthful recorder in fiction of New England village life. In several volumes of short stories and three or four novels she has caught the flavor of that life as no other author has; but when she writes on other subjects in other settings, she is usually less distinguished. Yet the rural New England of which she wrote was in the lowest ebb of its cultural history. Only the memories of its old vigor remained. The Civil War, the westward migrations, and industry had drained the countryside of much of its population. The Calvinist religion, though by no means extinct, was yielding its hold to Unitarianism or to indifference. Swelling numbers of Irish, French-Canadian, and other newcomers were successfully competing with the Yankee inhabitants as farmers, diluting the old way of life with different, though not necessarily inferior, customs and outlooks. But much of the old endured—especially in the more remote and smaller communities—and remains, often in an amalgamation with the new. Of this remnant, persistent even in the face of overwhelming change, Freeman wrote, and in doing so she described the very essence of the New England character, both in its individual and in its social aspects. But before examining her writing, one must take a closer look at the place and times that provided her material.

"Daniel Webster addressed 15,000 here"

In a small clearing at the height of land on the mountain road between Arlington and Stratton in southern Vermont, a plaque embedded in a boulder bears the words: "Daniel Webster addressed 15,000 here." The event occurred during the Log Cabin and Hard Cider Campaign of 1840; the crowd came from farms and villages on either side of the mountains. Today the spot is in the midst of a national forest, with only skiing resorts and recreational cabins anywhere near it. The farmlands have since been devoured by the forests and the villages depopulated. Most of the inhabitants vanished long ago into Civil War graves, westward to the prairies or the California goldfields, or downcountry to the manufacturing cities. Much of Vermont and, indeed, much of the hill country all over New England suffered a similar fate.

In the same county in which Webster drew such a throng is situated Brattleboro, the home of Freeman from the age of fourteen to thirty-one. In this Connecticut River Valley town she learned the craft of writing, and there and in the adjacent countryside she found the subjects for many of her best stories and novels. Brattleboro was somewhat of an oasis in a desert of decay. But to live in that area in the years closely following the Civil War was to live in the midst of a demoralized and disintegrating society. The physical evidence was everywhere. Even today the past haunts the hills of all New England like a spectral army. A hiker along the footpaths or abandoned roads of any of a hundred upland townships will find the vestiges of vanished populations—mile after mile of stone walls interlacing forests already over a hundred years old; isolated cellar holes or whole villages of them with lilac bushes growing alongside and apple trees ungrafted for generations and yielding a fruit as bitter as the disappointment of the settlers who lived and failed there and then moved on; graveyards, fenced perhaps with granite slabs ten feet long but, even so, inadequate to fend off the intruding forest and underbrush—everywhere the tokens but not the actuality of a once thronging, hopeful life.[1]

"The Terminal Moraine"

The people who remained after the various migrations are those about whom Freeman wrote—the people whom Fred Pattee described as representing "the terminal moraine of New England Puritanism."[2] What manner of men and women were these who persisted doggedly on rocky hill-farms and in remote villages far up the narrow valleys of the back country? Their parents and grandparents, those settlers who had come from the older areas of the older states, were of course of Puritan stock of the sturdiest and stubbornest religious faith. The Calvinist doctrines of election and of the perseverance of saints must have played a part in enabling such persons to persist. "Endurance" was a favorite among Puritan names because it was a favorite Puritan virtue and a useful one in the settlement of the wilderness. But the settlers' belief that they probably were among God's chosen people, predestined to salvation, must also have supported them in circumstances that would defeat less favored persons. The human will and God's predestination when allied would be invincible, for the human will is then no less than an expression of God's. Even after the need for superhuman endurance no longer existed, one's trust in the invincibility of one's will, when it was thought to coincide with God's, persisted. Sometimes this lingering willpower found useful outlets. Sometimes—frequently in Freeman's stories—it exerted itself on ignoble goals, mere whims and eccentricities, with all the force with which it had been directed against the hostile wilderness when its goal was the establishment of the New Jerusalem in New England.

One of Freeman's purposes was to exhibit in her writings these latter-day manifestations of the Calvinist will, just as Ellen Glasgow explored similar vestiges in the Presbyterian Calvinists of western Virginia. Glasgow, to be sure, celebrated the more positive aspects of the Calvinist will—the "vein of iron," the inflexible endurance, that carried her Virginians through the catastrophes of the modern world. Freeman specialized, though not exclusively, in the almost pathological manifestations of the overdeveloped will deprived of a worthwhile channel for its powers. She saw much of residual Calvinism as a chaotic deposit of flinty, fruitless irrelevancies. Glasgow saw it as a continuing important influence in American life, always serviceable for survival, whether in Indian wars or the Great Depression.

Yet the New England countryside in Freeman's youth had not been totally drained of its best stock. In certain communities shiftlessness, decay, and inbreeding were the order. But other communities retained some of the old standards along with people of character who strove to perpetuate the tradition of hard work, thrift, and righteousness. The schools and academies continued to teach the three R's and the classics. The churches continued to preach only a slightly watered-down orthodoxy. Some towns spent more money on their poorhouses than on their roads, but the struggle to stay out of the poorhouse—not "to go on the town," as the saying was—gave added incentive for a parsimonious, hard-working way of life. The aims had become petty when compared to those of the pioneer days, but they were still compelling enough to keep many people of simple character from total moral collapse and to keep more complicated persons from anything worse than oddness. Wisely, Freeman usually chose not to write about moral degenerates. She was always on the look-out for persons who rose above the apparent dullness of their lives, and her search was often successful, sometimes resulting in the discovery of a truly admirable, though perhaps eccentric, character.

The New England Town

To understand Freeman's best works one must know the social and political aspects of the New England towns in which they are set. To begin, one may note a remarkable similarity among New England towns in their physical arrangements, in the ideals they strive to uphold, and in the character traits they nurture. One may choose an island town on the Maine Coast, a Champlain Valley town in Vermont, or a hill town in Connecticut; and one will find that the similarities among them far outnumber the differences.

The town itself is frequently comprised of several villages, which, along with the intervening countryside, are under the same government. The village that contains the town offices is usually near the center of the township and is the most important in other respects, containing the largest churches, schools, and shops. This central village is generally located at a crossroads, or perhaps around a common or "green." Here, apart from the public buildings, are the residences of the professional persons and the shopkeepers. But some of the dwellings are farmhouses, their meadows and pastures extending beyond the village streets. Stretching outward are roads to the outlying parts of the township.

Presiding over the religious, intellectual, and political life of the town are a set of popularly elected or appointed dignitaries. The churches have their pastors and deacons, congregationally chosen, to supervise the spiritual welfare of the citizens. The secular government rests in the town meeting, made up of all voting citizens. Each year, usually in March, the voters meet to discuss community affairs and to delegate their powers to elected officials: a panel of three to five or more selectmen, who are the general executors of the town laws; a road commissioner, who keeps the town highways passable; a clerk, who records vital statistics and keeps the town records; a treasurer; a constable; and a variety of other functionaries, such as an overseer of the poor, a fence-viewer, and a keeper of weights and measures. Lastly, the meeting elects a school board to maintain school buildings, hire and fire teachers, and administer school finances.

These are the basic characteristics of the New England town as it has existed since earliest colonial times, though of course certain changes have occurred. At present some of the lesser officials are no longer needed; state and federal governments have taken over in several matters formerly controlled by the towns; and regional schools have made education less of a neighborhood affair. But the most important changes, which came along after Freeman left New England, were those occasioned by the advent of women's suffrage, enabling women to vote in town meeting and hold office.

The effects of such a closely knit community structure are obvious. Through the churches and schools the values and mores of the group are inculcated early and firmly into every child. Feelings of security are undoubtedly strengthened by such homogeneity. But also strengthened is a concern for what others think. Since one of the values is self-reliance, an area of conflict appears: if one is not independent in thought and action, the community frowns; but if one's independence leads to a flaunting of other established values, the community disapproves. With such conflicts many of Freeman's stories deal. The conflicts, as will be seen, become intricate when they occur in a person endowed with a Calvinistically trained conscience and will—a will whose direction is conceived of as revealing one's relation to God and one's chances of salvation.

Randolph, Massachusetts

Into such a community—Randolph, Massachusetts—Freeman was born on 31 October 1852. Though only fourteen miles from the center of Boston, Randolph was in those days a typical rural New England town. It was, moreover, one of the towns that in the first years of the republic had peopled the settlements in the northern states of Vermont, New Hampshire, and Maine. Being in an old district of New England, it was prototypical. Closely knit racially and culturally, still church-centered, agricultural right up to its main street, it differed only in that it possessed more industry than the more remote towns. In the 1850s Randolph had produced a million dollars worth of shoes annually, many of them for the Australian market. Manufacturing was carried on in small factories and in little sheds in the yards of shoemakers' houses on a domestic-industry basis. But the days of domestic crafts were numbered. In the 1860s the Australian market vanished, and the local industry became concentrated in larger mills, notably at nearby Brockton. By the time Freeman was twelve years old, Randolph had gone the way of many small New England mill towns, where deserted factories were as common as abandoned farms. In its farming, too, Randolph suffered severely, though not as disastrously as the less fertile hill towns.

Freeman's parents were both natives of Randolph. Her father, Warren Wilkins, was connected on both sides with ancient and honored Salem families. Like Hawthorne, Freeman numbered among her forebears an ancestor involved in the witchcraft delusion of the seventeenth century; in her play *Giles Corey, Yeoman* she wrote about the persecution of witches. By trade Warren Wilkins was a carpenter, a housebuilder, with considerable talent as an architect; he was reputedly an overly conscientious man, sensitive, usually cheerful, but given to occasional somber moods. Freeman's mother, née Eleanor Lothrop, could also trace her descent on both sides from New England settlers of the 1640s. Her father, a housepainter, was a man of considerable means.

When Freeman was born, her parents were living in a new house on South Main Street in Randolph. There had been a previous baby who had died in infancy. Born a few years after Freeman was a brother who died at the age of three. A sister, seven years her junior, survived to the age of seventeen. Not a strong child herself, Freeman was naturally the object of the doting care of parents whose children had a propensity to illness. In addition, she was pretty and winsome and seems to have been rather spoiled. Yet the Puritan tradition of rearing children had not so far weakened as to exempt her from a strict code of behavior. Obedience certainly was the rule at home, church, and school, as were the virtues of thrift, honesty, temperance, and piety.

The Sabbaths were observed in the Wilkins household with all the old-time rigidity, for both parents were orthodox Congregationalists. Religious activities engrossed all of Sunday: 10:30 to 12:00, worship and sermon; 12:00 to 1:00, Sunday School; 2:00 to 3:00, preaching service; 4:00 to 5:00, a young people's service; 7:00 to 8:00, prayer meeting. A program like this, attended in its entirety by the faithful and their families, ensured that over the years a child would become thoroughly familiar with the Bible and its Calvinist interpretations, with church dogma, and with the application of scriptural and doctrinal teachings to daily living. By adulthood a churchgoer in a New England town of something over a hundred years ago would be well-grounded in practical and theoretical theology. In every family, religion was discussed, even among the hired help; and the Wilkins family was no exception. If, as her biographer Edward Foster says, Freeman as a young child could not understand fully the niceties of doctrine discussed in her hearing, "she must at least have learned that theology in her family was bound up with deep personal feelings and that somehow faith and goodness were related to one's material success in the world. In her house, it was always assumed that the poverty of the poor was punishment for sin."[3]

For the thirty years prior to Freeman's birth the pulpit in the Randolph Congregational Church had been occupied by a pastor who preached only a slightly diluted Calvinism. There followed two preachers who were tainted with liberalism. Most important in Freeman's spiritual life was the Reverend John C. Labaree, who took the pastorate at Randolph in 1865 and preached an orthodoxy largely shorn not only of the terror but of the vigor of Calvinism. He held to many of the old conceptions—original sin, regeneration and sanctification of the soul through the grace of God operating as the Holy Comforter, justification before God, and remissions of sins exclusively through the atonement of Christ. But the pivotal Calvinist doctrine of election was played down in Dr. Labaree's church; nor was there any harping on, or belief in, the wrathful nature of God in dealing with sinners, the prospect of eternal hellfire for those not chosen for salvation, or the necessity of adoring the God that might well have predestined one from before one's birth to inevitable damnation. This moderate, rather kindly, religion is the one that Freeman adopted for herself. But she knew also, from her parents and their generation, the old-time religion handed down from the Puritan forefathers.

School probably influenced Freeman less profoundly or lastingly than did the church. Beginning at the age of seven, she attended the common school in Randolph. Naturally bright and receiving from her teacher the same deference that she was used to at home, she soon earned from her fellow pupils the titles "stuck-up," "teacher's partial," and "little dolly-pinky-rosy."[4] In short, she was accorded the usual treatment experienced by an exceptional child at school: the teacher petted her, and the children hated her. Thrown back on herself, she must have come to value more and more the rewards of self-reliance as well as to understand its pains. In numerous stories she later described the struggles of strong-willed individualists in a disapproving and jeering community. The fact that the protagonists in these stories find peace of mind only when they return to the village norm suggests that Freeman may have suffered from her childhood ostracism, however bravely she may have shrugged it off.

Not that Freeman, as a girl, was entirely without playmates; early in childhood, indeed, she made one friendship that survived until the intervention of death. This friendship was with Mary Wales, the daughter of a Randolph farmer whose hundred acres fronted on the main street not far from the school. After classes, the two girls often spent long hours at the farmhouse. Here Freeman learned about farm life both in the fields and barns and in the housewife's kitchen—knowledge that supplied her with details and insights for numerous writings. Much later, from 1884 to 1901, she lived in the Wales home as a friend and boarder.

Growing up in Randolph made Freeman a New England village woman, whatever she might become or wherever she might live later. Fixed in her memory from childhood were the great elm-shaded houses along Main Street, the school, church, and culture that they preserved, the long snowy winters, the raw bleak springs, the brief simmering summers, and the autumn ablaze with crimson and yellow. Here she learned of the parsimony of the peddlers hawking their pots from door to door, the meanness of village gossip purveyed in whispers in stove-heated kitchens, and the unsung heroism of those who defied gossip to be true to themselves, however queer or warped they might be. Here also she knew the security of living in a homogeneous community, in which most of one's acquaintances and neighbors were of the same Anglo-Saxon stock, subscribed to the same ancestral credos and codes of behavior, spoke the same dialect of the same language, and knew one another's family histories for generations back. And here she learned of the insecurity that homogeneity can foster—not only fear of what people may think or say, but dread of the complete or partial exclusion that comes with nonconformity, all the timidities that Emerson and Thoreau, themselves New England villagers by choice, strove to exorcise in such essays as "Self-Reliance" and "Civil Disobedience."

Brattleboro, Vermont

In 1867 Warren Wilkins, no longer able to make a good living in Randolph, moved to Brattleboro, Vermont, where he intended to establish a drygoods store in partnership with a friend. Though Wilkins had bought a building lot in a fashionable residential section, he settled his family in a small cottage near the common. Nearby was the Vermont Insane Asylum, which furnished Freeman with glimpses of personality distortions suggestive of ones she later wrote about. Now fifteen, she attended the public high school, where she took the usual courses in Latin, natural philosophy, mathematics, and rhetoric. She also contributed to the elocution recitations presented by the students and wrote skits for production at school entertainments.

Brattleboro, a fashionable spa before the Civil War, was still a town with some pretense to cultural importance. Among its many old and respected families were the Tylers, true Brahmins who had produced an impressive roster of jurists and clergymen and even one author, the playwright Royall Tyler. In Freeman's time the arts were cultivated there, and the life of the mind and the spirit was well-nurtured by an active lyceum, a first-rate bookstore, and a well-known orchestra under the direction of Christian Schuster.

Among the notable native personages were the sculptor John Larkin Mead, Jr., the painters William Morris Hunt and Robert G. Hardie, and the architect Richard Hunt. In belles lettres, in addition to Freeman herself, the town could claim the essayist Samuel M. Crothers and, for several years, Rudyard Kipling, who had married a Brattleboro woman, Caroline Balestier, a friend of Freeman's. Though Kipling had come to Brattleboro after Freeman had returned to Randolph, she met him there on subsequent visits. A neighbor of the Wilkins family was the writer Colonel T. W. Higginson's sister Anna, who presided over a "salon" of the artists and people of culture in the town, though Freeman was either too timid or too proud to force herself into this circle.

In 1870 Freeman graduated from high school and entered Mount Holyoke Female Seminary. But life there was too rigorous for her health, and she left after a year. One thing that Mount Holyoke could be counted on doing, as those who know the life of Emily Dickinson will recall, was to sharpen the religious sensitivities of its students. Indeed, one of its avowed purposes was to bring to conversion every girl who had not previously had that experience. Whether a girl resisted, as did Dickinson, or was already converted, as was Freeman, the hammering away at the collective student conscience at prayer meetings and church services, not to mention annual revivals, could only intensify whatever religious feelings one might have. It was not by chance that many Mount Holyoke girls became missionaries' wives. But, like Dickinson, Freeman found that a year in this atmosphere was all she could endure. After leaving Mount Holyoke, she returned to Vermont and spent the following year taking courses at a girls' seminary in West Brattleboro. Thus ended her formal education. But she was an avid reader, though a somewhat haphazard one. She and her friend Evelyn Sawyer of nearby Newfane read and discussed Goethe, Emerson, Thoreau, Dickens, Thackeray, Poe, Harriet Beecher Stowe, and Sarah Orne Jewett.

In 1873 Freeman met Hanson Tyler, a navy ensign on leave home after a tour of duty in Havana. She fell deeply in love with him, but he did not return her feelings strongly enough to prompt a proposal of marriage. Like many single women in her stories, Freeman cherished her unrequited love through middle age, even after Tyler himself had married. Until her death she kept a photograph of him and buttons from his uniform, and in her last years she had these buttons sewn onto her dressing gown.[5]

Also in 1873, a time of business depression, Warren Wilkins was forced to sell his drygoods store and return to his former trade of carpentry. He had previously given up his plan of building a house for his family on the site he had purchased on first coming to Brattleboro. To help financially, Freeman tried teaching in a school for girls, but quit after a year because she found herself unsuited for the work by either interest or ability. For a time she thought of becoming an artist, inspired perhaps by the Hunts and John Larkin Mead. Later her stories had pictorial qualities in their descriptions and in their grouping of characters, but for actual painting she had little talent. Soon, for want of anything else to do, she began to write, at first mainly poetry. Her initial efforts, religious in theme, were not offered for publication. A little later she turned to children's verse, some of which she was able to place without pay in an obscure Fall River magazine. Not for years did her writing earn any money. Yet she had found her vocation and proceeded to fill a box with manuscripts and rejection slips.

In 1876 came a devastating blow: Freeman's sister Anna, who was engaged to one of Christian Schuster's musicians, died at the age of seventeen. Meanwhile, the father's financial position continued to deteriorate. In 1877 the family moved into the household of the Reverend Thomas Pickman Tyler, Hanson Tyler's father, where Freeman's mother served as housekeeper. Many of Freeman's fictional characters regarded such subserviency as the ultimate disgrace that could befall them. The pride of the Wilkinses, who suspected that poverty was the punishment for sin, must have been badly bruised. In addition, for Freeman this relationship with the parents of the man she loved must have been hard to bear. However, the family remained on terms of social equality with the Tylers in the tradition of rural New England, where servants were called "help" and often ate at the table with their employers. With one of the Tylers, Aunt Bessie Tyler Billings, Free-

man was on terms of close friendship. The two took frequent drives
together into the country around Brattleboro, especially up the Connecticut and West River valleys, where the depopulated villages and
crumbling, empty farmhouses cast a gloom on the bright, green beauty
of the hills—excursions that provided Freeman with the settings, the
atmosphere, and the moods that appear in her best work.

All her life Freeman had fond memories of her years at Brattleboro.
She often recalled the great beauty of its location and vividly remem-
bered watching the moon rise above the mountain across the Connecticut River. "Sometimes I wonder," she wrote to Fred Lewis Pattee, "if
the marvelous beauty of that locality was not largely instrumental in
making me try to achieve anything."[6] She had good memories, too, of
her schooling there and of "the splendid humanity of Brattleboro people."[7] It was in Brattleboro that she first fully awakened to the beauty
of nature, formed some of her most important friendships, and first
experienced love for a man. There also she made her early acquaintance
with the world of books and did her first writing. Shortly before her
death she wrote to a friend that Brattleboro became part of herself.[8]
Doubtless, also, the profound feelings that the natural beauty of the
region aroused in her germinated in the nature mysticism revealed in
many of her writings.

"Faithful, hopeful, and independent work"

Residence with the Reverend Pickman Tyler ended abruptly with
the death of Freeman's mother at the age of fifty-three. The shock was
brutal, for Freeman had always depended on her mother's strength.
Moving to new quarters, she kept up her morale by keeping house for
her father and by continuing her writing. Finally in 1881 she received
her first payment as an author, ten dollars for the ballad "The Beggar
King" that she had placed in the children's magazine *Wide Awake*. The
poem runs to some fifty stanzas that tell a story in continuation of the
nursery rhyme:

> Hark! Hark! Hark! The dogs do bark!
>   The beggars have come to town;
>   Some in rags and some in tags,
>   And some in velvet gowns.[9]

Freeman's first book, *Decorative Plaques,* with illustrations by George
F. Barnes, consisted of verse previously published in *Wide Awake* and

appeared in 1883. Her next two books—*The Cow with the Golden Horns and Other Stories* (1884) and *The Adventures of Anne: Stories of Colonial Times* (1886)—were also for children. As a writer for children both in verse and in prose, Freeman had a true talent, and as early as 1882 she was contributing to *St. Nicholas,* the best of all children's magazines.

In January 1882 Freeman won a fifty-dollar prize from the *Boston Sunday Budget* with her first story for adults, "The Shadow Family," no copy of which either in print or in manuscript has survived. In the autumn of that same year her father, in poor health, went to Gainesville, Florida, where he had found employment in construction work. That winter in Brattleboro Freeman wrote the first story of those later to be included in her first major book, *A Humble Romance and Other Stories* (1887). This story, "Two Old Lovers," recounts a situation common in the writing of Freeman and of other writers about rural New England—a love affair that prolongs itself from the youth to the old age of the lovers but never culminates in marriage. Her treatment of the subject is distinctive, however, and presaged her manner in the years to follow. The setting, a small, decaying mill town suggestive of Randolph, is sketched with an accuracy that conveys painfully its stagnation and drabness. The male lover, David Emmons, who is the weaker of the pair, as is usual in Freeman's fiction, is the victim of total atrophy of will. The story is, in fact, a study of the workings of the will, or lack of will, in the two main characters—and this theme is also highly representative of Freeman's work. David Emmons has simply lacked the willpower to propose to his sweetheart, Maria Brewster; and after half a lifetime of indecision he dies without asking the question. Maria all along has displayed excessive patience and devotion that in themselves are abnormalities. As her tongue-tied lover grows older and feebler, she cooks for him. She is by his bedside at his death, when he says: "Maria, I'm—dyin', an'—I allers meant to—have asked you—to—marry me."[10] As one critic has written, both David and Maria exemplify "a pitiful caricature of people who let life happen to them without question. . . ,"[11] which is the state that many of Freeman's New England villagers have sunk to. Further, the lifelong courtship of the couple, who had never held hands or kissed, would seem to stem from a revulsion against their sexuality, the energies of which David has directed into gardening and Maria into cooking.[12] Though the reader may smile wryly at the spectacle of these grotesque "lovers," the final impression is one of sadness.

Freeman had sent the manuscript of "Two Old Lovers" to Mary

Louise Booth, editor of *Harper's Bazar*. As soon as Booth saw the handwriting, which resembled a child's, she decided to reject the story. But looking a little more closely, she became interested, and after three readings accepted it. Until her death in 1889 Booth was Freeman's literary advisor and close friend. The story brought its author twenty-five dollars and a strong sense of accomplishment. Her enthusiasm for writing, now intensified, scarcely slackened for the next forty years. The story was a landmark in her development because it was the first to employ successfully the material she knew best—aspects of life in a village like the one in which she had grown up and persons like ones she had known all her life. "A young writer," she advised many years later, "should follow the safe course of writing only about those subjects she knows thoroughly, and concerning which she trusts her own convictions. . . . She should make her own patterns and found her own school. . . . The keynote of the whole is, as in every undertaking in this world, faithful, hopeful, and independent work."[13]

Freeman's joy at the *Harper's Bazar* acceptance was soon dampened. A few months later word came that her father had died in Florida. Burial took place in the family plot in Randolph, where her sister and now both her parents had been buried within six years—a succession of losses that, when added to her disappointment with Hanson Tyler, had a profound effect upon her for the rest of her life. Like many spinsters in her fiction she was left alone with only her beloved cat Augustus. After the interment she returned to Brattleboro, remaining there until the end of the year. *Harper's Bazar* in the meantime published three more of her stories. The following summer she took up permanent residence with her former playmate Mary Wales in the old farmhouse she had known so well as a child.

A Clutch of Early Poems

During her last years in Brattleboro Freeman also wrote poems for an adult readership, four of of which appeared in the *Century Magazine*. The first, entitled "Sweet Phyllis, A Pastoral" (1882), is a graceful trifle about a shepherdess and her swain. It testifies to Freeman's facility with rhyme and meter, and it caused Brattleboro readers of the prestigious *Century* to take notice of her existence. The next to appear in the *Century* was "Boy's-Love" (1883), again adroitly written, about a girl who unsuccessfully seeks a lover through the use of the magical power of the herb named in the title. This was followed in 1884 by

"It Was a Lass," in which a girl seeks love but finds it in none of the
lads she meets and concludes that it exists nowhere but in her own
heart. These poems appeared in a section of the magazine headed "Bric-
à-Brac" and should not be taken very seriously. Yet each is about a girl
seeking a lover, and in only the first is she successful. We know that
Hanson Tyler was much on Freeman's mind at this time and that her
love for him was unrequited. Her own disappointment may have been
reflected in these poems.

The fourth of the *Century* poems, "A Maiden Lady" (1885), is more
interesting than the others, forming a sequel and a culmination to
them and echoing themes and moods of many of the stories she was
writing at the time or would write later:

> Of a summer afternoon,
> In her parlor window there,
> She would sit, her meek face showing
> Delicately long and fair,
> Sewing on some dainty garment, no one ever saw her wear.
>
> She'd be dressed in cool old muslin
> With a lilac pattern dim;
> Full soft skirt, and pointed body
> Cut severely straight and prim—
> Maiden-dress and maiden lady, sober, delicate and prim.
>
> She seemed not with love acquainted;
> Half too fine to hold him dear.
> Folk spoke shyly of love-matters,
> With this maiden lady near,
> With a feeling it were converse hardly suited to her ear.
>
> When she cried, poor, shy old maiden,
> Her artless secret saw the sun:—
> She had been with love acquainted,
> Always, just like any one:—
> But had kept him in a closet hidden, as a skeleton.[14]

When this poem was published Freeman was thirty-three; already, in
her day, she could be considered an old maid. On the surface the
"maiden lady" in the poem is completely the stereotypical spinster—
unobtrusively dressed, prim, meek, innocent of even the knowledge of

love, and asexual. Her occupation, like that of many single women whether rich or poor in Freeman's fiction, is to sit by a window and watch the world as it passes her by. But the last three lines, which provide the title for a recent perceptive dissertation on Freeman, completely invalidate the stereotype conveyed by the rest of the poem. The "maiden lady" was "with love acquainted . . . but had kept him in a closet hidden, as a skeleton." She had not been, and was not now, without her sexuality, but for reasons of her own, perhaps for fear of ridicule, had chosen to present herself to the world in the role it expected of her. It was a role that Freeman probably resented, because to others it seemed to fit her (she was later popularly associated with her own fictional "New England Nun"). Twenty years after she wrote the poem, in "The Old Maid Aunt" chapter of the cooperative novel *The Whole Family,* she took great pleasure in creating a spinster who did not hide her sexuality or live and dress according to the world's expectations. [15]

In a letter, the literary historian Fred Lewis Pattee told Freeman that he admired her "child verse" and the *vers de société,* as he called it, that she had contributed to the *Century,* and he inquired if she had "written other verse"; he added, "I hope so. The lyric Gods certainly were good to you and I hope you have not disappointed them." Freeman's reply was terse. She could make more money writing fiction, and she needed money to support herself and her aunt. [16] However, she did occasionally write verse for most of the rest of her life. The *Century* poems are probably her best, though it is a question whether they warrant Pattee's high praise.

Chapter Two
A Humble Romance and Other Stories

Though Freeman often returned to Brattleboro on visits, she never made her home there again after 1884. Yet the Brattleboro years left an indelible mark on her writing. A careful reading of her early stories and novels reveals that a large proportion of them have Vermont settings, not so much Brattleboro as the surrounding countryside. The characters, too, in her writing of this period, with their taciturnity, their fierce independence, and their self-will, are more suggestive of Vermont than eastern Massachusetts. An editor, in fact, suggested that Freeman's book *A Humble Romance and Other Stories* be entitled *Green Mountain Stories.*[1] Yet Freeman's stories, apart from their strictly New England flavor, are not for the most part closely localized. She knew both the Vermont and Massachusetts villagers and country people, and she found the likenesses between the two to be much more noticeable than the differences. Later, as the immediacy of the Vermont years wore off, she drifted more into settings reminiscent of Randolph, but the people she wrote about remained much the same.

"And *they* are American"

In 1887 the stories Freeman had written for *Harper's New Monthly* and *Harper's Bazar* were collected in a volume of over four hundred pages entitled *A Humble Romance and Other Stories*. One of her most successful and enduring books, it contains a half dozen or so stories that she never surpassed either in narrative skill or in psychological insight. For an Edinburgh edition of the first fourteen selections in the book she wrote in 1889 a brief preface stating her purpose:

These little stories were written about the village people of New England. They are studies of the descendants of the Massachusetts Bay colonists, in

16

whom can still be seen traces of those features of will and conscience, so strong as to be almost exaggerations and deformities, which characterised their ancestors.

These traces are, however, more evident among the older people; among the younger, they are dimmer and more modified. It therefore seems better worth the while to try to preserve in literature still more of this old and probably disappearing type of New England character, although it has been done with the best results by other American authors.[2]

The "other American authors" were probably Hawthorne, Jewett, Stowe, and Rose Terry Cooke; but Freeman need not have been so self-effacing, for in her unique manner of dealing with her subject matter she was in no way their inferior.

The stories in *A Humble Romance* are developed in an atmosphere of decay common at the time to most up-country New England villages. Freeman had become an important interpreter of New England life under conditions of decline, and her fiction was later cited in sociological articles. Rollin Lynde Hartt, for example, in a two-part study published in the *Atlantic Monthly* in April and May of 1899 under the title "A New England Hill Town," gave her the status of an authority. The articles are not only a testimony to her accuracy as a reporter, but they give interesting factual insights into the milieu that she had made her specialty.

The town that Hartt described is in the hills of western Massachusetts, a region closely similar to the southern Green Mountains where Freeman had lived. "The rural environment," Hartt wrote, "is psychologically extravagant. It tends to extremes. A man carries himself out to his logical conclusions; he becomes a concentrated essence of himself."[3] Inbreeding, he found, creates exaggerated types: misers, hermits, and a great assortment of other eccentrics, as well as mental and physical defectives. The hill towns, he thought, were anachronisms, despite the efforts of older people to keep them alive. They were communities without hope, harboring the ambitionless and the children of the ambitionless. Most deplorable and ruinous was the absence of contact with the outside world. In families in which a child had gone to college or in which a city person has been welcomed, vitality might return—which would indicate that, like Freeman, Hartt considered the chief shortcomings of these towns to be cultural rather than hereditary, in spite of his references to inbreeding. At any rate, of all of those who had attempted to depict life in these forgotten towns, Hartt

considered that Freeman had been by far the most truthful. Yet Freeman, when queried as to the accuracy of Hartt's article, replied: "I
know nothing whatever about the hill towns"[4]—a disclaimer that it is
difficult to take seriously.

Rudyard Kipling, who had lived in Brattleboro during the 1890s
and perhaps knew Freeman's stories (though he does not cite them),
wrote in *Something of Myself* (1937) even more somberly than Hartt:
"The country was large-boned, mountainous, wooded, and divided
into farms of from fifty to two hundred barren acres. Roads, sketched
in dirt, connected white clap-boarded houses, where the older members of the families made shift to hold down the eating mortgages. The
younger folk had gone elsewhere. There were many abandoned houses
too; some decaying where they stood; others already reduced to a stone
chimney-stack or mere green dimples still held by an undefeated lilac
bush."[5] Kipling spoke also of the taciturnity and suspiciousness of the
New England country folk, who accepted him only because his wife
was a Vermonter. The lives on the farms he described as lonely and
sterile: "What might have become characters, powers, and attributes
perverted themselves in that desolation as cankered trees throw out
branches akimbo, and strange faiths and cruelties, born of solitude to
the edge of insanity, flourished like lichen on sick bark."[6] Yet—and
this is important—Kipling had feelings other than pity or condemnation for the Vermont farmers. In a dispatch to the London *Times* of
29 November 1892, he pictured them as superior to the distraught
city people who flock into the countryside each summer to recuperate
from the ravages of their hectic living during the rest of the year—
people who will never achieve the steadfastness, the repose, and the
purposefulness of their rustic neighbors, of whom Kipling writes in
concluding his article, "And *they* are American."[7]

Of these bedrock people, warped and eccentric though many of them
were, Freeman wrote in *A Humble Romance* and in most of her later
books. Their endurance and what Ellen Glasgow, writing of their
coreligionists in Virginia, called their fortitude are their salient
characteristics. In dealing at times with these virtues in excessive manifestations—with diseases of the will—Freeman in no way underrates
the dignity and significance of lives led without surrender or thought
of it, under severe stress and adversity. As a result, like Robert Frost,
whose vision of New England character William Dean Howells as early
as 1915 compared to hers,[8] Freeman never permits the merely sordid,
the "realistic," to becloud the entire picture.

The Possibility of "Beauty and Grace"

The title story in *A Humble Romance* presents two lonely, obscure people who manage to generate beauty and happiness in their commonplace lives. Sally, an orphan brought up as a servant girl by an exacting and mean-tempered village woman, suddenly belies her reputation for mousy timorousness by walking out of her mistress's kitchen and marrying a tinker who happens by in the course of his rounds. The potentiality of revolt in meek and downtrodden natures is a favorite theme with Freeman; she relates it to a theme of the unpredictability and limitless capacities of the human will. Sally makes her choice in a matter of minutes, while her mistress is in the attic hunting up old rags with which to pay the tinker. More important, Freeman makes this sudden revolt plausible, by presenting it not only as a revolt but also as a conversion from submission to self-fulfillment. The change is entirely within Sally, and it takes place with no enhanced feelings of rancor, which indeed she has never felt, toward her employer. She simply decides to leave one sort of life for another. Heroics play no part in the process:

Whether it was by the grace of God, or an inheritance from some far-off Puritan ancestor, the fire in whose veins had not burned low, she could see, if she saw nothing else, the distinction between right and wrong with awful plainness. Nobody had ever called her anything but a *good* girl. It was said with a disparagement, maybe, but it was always "a good girl." . . . She looked at her lover, and began to believe in him, and as soon as she began to believe in him—poor, unattractive, ignorant little thing that she was!—she began to love just like other girls. (6–7)

Many of Freeman's browbeaten people explode into violent revolt, malicious and destructive. But there is nothing violent about Sally's change, and perhaps that is why it is so final.

Thus, surprisingly to herself as much as to others, Sally proves capable of making and acting upon a momentous decision. Other potentialities now emerge. Her honest tinker husband, who loves Sally and to whom she is devoted, discovers that his first wife, who long ago had left him and whom he thought dead, is in fact alive. When the man she had run off with in turn deserted her, she sought out her husband and demanded his support on pain of his being exposed as a bigamist.

The tinker departs, leaving Sally a letter promising that he will return if he is ever able to and urging her to "bear up." He does not explain why or to what destination he is leaving. But Sally's faith in the husband with whom she has found a new and better life is more than sufficient to enable her merely to "bear up." Endurance and patience are part of her heritage, as well as initiative. During the years her husband is away, the captive of his former unhappiness, she takes over his peddling, driving his wagon around the countryside. When he is finally released by the death of his wife, he returns and the two remarry with unimpaired love and undiminished gratefulness to life.

The story, especially in summary, may seem sentimental; but—what matters more—it may also be true to life. In both Randolph and Brattleboro Freeman had known girls who, like Sally, endured the interminable bleakness of a kitchen-maid's dollar-a-week servitude, and she had been well acquainted with the peddlers who in those days roamed the New England countryside. The question implicit in this and many of Freeman's stories is: Are such lives doomed to perpetual dreariness and insignificance, or can they be redeemed by qualities latent in the victims themselves? Freeman finds that "beauty and grace" (16) are possible even in such lives and are attainable in terms of values and forces inherent in the New England background. It is interesting that Sally, after her initial rebellion and her spell as a peddler—an activity unheard of and frowned upon for a woman in the later 1800s—relapses into her former submissiveness, becoming her husband's "little un" (24), as society and the editors of *Harper's Bazar* demanded of a wife. Yet she has twice demonstrated her ability to act independently of socially prescribed roles, and doubtless she would do so again if she found it necessary.

The possibility of "beauty and grace" may always be present, but it does not always materialize. Too often in Freeman's fiction a life is allowed to slip by without realization of its potential, and the Jamesian tragedy of the unfulfilled existence occurs. In their dealings with human motivations Henry James and Freeman have, in fact, much in common. James attributed the failure to attain fulfillment either to excessive independence of will, as with Daisy Miller or Isabel Archer, or to feebleness of will, as with Daisy's American lover Winterbourne or Isabel's cousin Ralph. And in James's work, as in Freeman's, the men are often weaker willed than the women. It is not surprising, therefore, that James followed Freeman's writing with interest.

Failure of Will

If Sally's chief strength is an unswerving determination, other characters in *A Humble Romance* are weak-willed to the point of aboulia. One such is Caroline Munson in "A Symphony in Lavender." She has lost her chance of whatever happiness marriage might bring because she cannot make up her mind as to the meaning of a dream. At the opening of the story she is an elderly and genteel spinster, living alone with an old servant in her ancestral mansion where she keeps up her pretentions as a charming hostess. From her own lips the reader learns that in her youth she had dreamed that she met a young man to whom she was first attached but for whom her feelings soon changed to disgust. Later, in real life, she meets a man who resembles the man in the dream. She finds him attractive and even comes to love him, but clouding her love is a consciousness of latent "horror of him" (46). When he proposes to her, the horror surfaces; he has become revolting to her and she regards him as evil. Of course she rejects him. But thenceforward she speculates as to whether her dream was an omen from God or a "nervous whim" (47). She can only hope it was the former, for in rejecting her lover she would have been acquiescing in divine will—ample justification, in the mind of a daughter of the Puritans, for any act, however unreasonable. But to Freeman, as to the reader, Caroline Munson's timidity—her failure to see the truth that she was afraid of marriage—has little to do with God. It stems from her own inner conflict. To live with her lilacs and her Bible and her constant prayers was easier than to live with a husband and accept the sexuality that religion and her upbringing had probably caused her to consider evil. At any rate, whether God or whim directed her decision, she lacks the firmness of purpose, the self-direction, that Sally was able to muster.[9]

The Pride of the Poor

Cases of enfeebled wills like Caroline's are common in Freeman's writings, an outstanding example being that of Louisa Ellis in "A New England Nun." But more frequently an excess rather than a deficiency of willpower blights the lives of Freeman's women in *A Humble Romance*. In "A Taste of Honey" a young woman, Inez, sets out to pay off the mortgage on the family farm that her father, now dead, had striven for a lifetime to free of debt. She refuses to marry until she has accomplished this purpose, though she has an eager lover. On the day she makes her final payment, this lover, weary of delay, marries another girl. Inez puts on a brave face and treats her mother to a taste of the honey that they had hitherto sold to help raise the mortgage money. The mother says to her daughter: "But I should think losin' your beau would take all the sweetness out of the honey." And Inez answers: "I guess there's a good many folks find it the same way with their honey in this world" (106).

It is not the loss of her undependable beau that has taken the sweetness out of Inez's honey, but her realization of the wrongness of sacrificing herself for a mortgage. But "the pitiful spectacle of her poor, dull father working all his life for such a small aim in such small ways, in vain, haunted her" (103). Pride for herself and for her dead, defeated father force her to carry on where he left off, even at the cost of the fulfillment of her womanhood. In this early volume Freeman was already vividly depicting the miseries of rural poverty and its psychological effects on its victims. Later she devoted whole novels to the subject, exploring more deeply the relationship between poverty and pride. At this early stage her probings did not go beyond the proverbial concept that the poor are very proud—and with a pride that sometimes, as with Inez, demands uncalled for sacrifices.

Another study of poverty in *A Humble Romance* occurs in "Old Lady Pingree," the story of an octogenerian of gentle birth who is permitted to take in boarders in her ancestral mansion, which the bank has long since taken over. She accepts charity but will not acknowledge it. Any gifts, say of food, must be left surreptitiously behind a door for her to pick up when no one, not even the donor, is looking. The one prop to her tottering pride is the eighty dollars that she has saved for her burial; for to be buried at the town's expense is the ultimate humiliation, comparable only to ending one's days at the poor farm. Unfortunately one of Old Lady Pingree's boarders dies before she does, leaving no funds for his funeral. Miss Pingree, acting as the village would expect of one of her breeding, promptly lends her own burial sum to the dead boarder's daughter; to do otherwise would totally demolish her self-respect. Later, when the bank sells part of her land to a railroad company, she is inveigled into accepting two hundred dollars against her own burial, not as a gift, as the bankers carefully point out (though it is a gift), but as rightfully hers because of an increase in the value of her land. She is entirely satisfied with this arrangement. Not only does it ensure her own respectable burial, but it permits her to do the gracious, ladylike act of dropping her claim to the eighty dollars she had loaned to the dead boarder's daughter.

Indeed, cajoling paupers into accepting help is one of the problems of village life as Freeman depicts it. Always the recipient must be made to feel that he or she is not the receiver of alms; the act of giving becomes an elaborate ritual in which the donor pretends that the needy are doing a favor by accepting gifts. Thus in the story "A Mistaken Charity," recently presented as a drama on public television, two elderly women, living wholly on the kindness of their neighbors, are insultingly critical of everything they receive. Were they grateful, they fear folks might consider them poor enough to be sent to the pauper's home.

The Ties of Place

The villager's attachment to home, no matter how drab, is the theme of several stories in *A Humble Romance*. In "Brakes and White Vi'lets" Marm Lawson lives with her granddaughter Levina in a house so damp and musty, because of its situation on wet ground, that the child becomes ill and has to be taken away to her father's house in a distant town. So strong are the bonds that attach the old woman to her own house and to the brakes and violets in its dooryard that she would rather live alone than with her son and granddaughter. On one occasion she sets out to visit them but gets no farther than the railroad station in the next village. When the train comes, she does not board it but spends the night in the station, returning the next morning by stagecoach to her home. Only on her deathbed does she see her son and Levina again. Human ties, though strong, are weaker with her than those of place. Marm Lawson's well-being, if not her sense of values, has been conditioned by the monotony of life in a mildewy house in a village ten miles from the railroad. She is no longer able to forgo dull habit for the love of a child. Dehumanization with her is far advanced. As a critic has observed, her "home has become a source of death rather than life."[10]

Overrefined Consciences

In other stories in *A Humble Romance* sensitivity exaggerated to the point of morbidity exerts a stunting effect. Sometimes the sensitivity arises from motives in themselves unexceptionable. Such is the case with Adoniram Dill in "In Butterfly Time." Forty years before the opening of the story, Adoniram had been on the point of marrying Rebecca Wheat. But one day, when the hilarity of his spirits got the better of him and he chased a butterfly in the Wheats' garden, Rebecca's mother made a disparaging remark. Adoniram, who had just experienced conversion and was striving to behave like a Christian, mistakenly assumed that Mrs. Wheat's remarks indicated that she did not like him and thus would prefer not to have her daughter marry him. Rather than go against the mother's wishes, he did what he thought was the Christian thing by breaking his engagement with Rebecca. Forty years of celibacy for him and Rebecca have ensued. Whether a fear of marriage may have underlain his hyperconscientiousness is open to question. At any rate, the waste of these years in terms of possible happiness and personal fulfillment is not diminished when the misunderstanding is finally cleared up and the two, now in their sixties, get married.

Another victim of an overrefined conscience is Martha Patch in "An Honest Soul." Martha, one of the scores of lonely, impoverished seamstresses who inhabit Freeman's pages, one day receives orders for patchwork quilts from two customers who leave bundles of rags for her to work with. When she has completed the quilts, for each of which she will receive one dollar, she discovers that in one of them she has used a scrap of cloth belonging to the other customer. She tears both quilts apart and resews them, only to find that she has again made a similar error, which she again unhesitatingly rectifies by redoing both quilts. By this time, having earned no money, she has not eaten for several days. When she finally completes the quilts and is about to deliver them, she faints and lies unconscious on her floor until a neighbor rescues her. Freeman speculates: "It is a hard question to decide, whether there were any real merit in such finely strained honesty, or whether it were really a case of morbid conscientiousness. Perhaps the old woman, inheriting very likely her father's scruples, had had them so intensified by age and childlessness that they had become a little off the bias of reason" (86). Like the romancers of the Middle Ages who would pose to their listeners some question of conduct to be answered with reference to the code of courtly love, Freeman, half-humorously perhaps, leaves the reader with a question of conscience to be resolved in terms of the religion of John Calvin as modified by three hundred years of transplantation in New England. But the reader may put the question in different terms: Was not Martha's conscience the only basis for self-respect left to this destitute woman whom life had passed by in her shabby little cottage in a run-down New England village?

Setness of Will

A sheer fixation of will—whether right or wrong in its direction— is another crippling trait among the people in *A Humble Romance*. "On the Walpole Road" is the story of a man and woman afflicted with this defect. The woman, because of family pressure, marries the man despite her love for another. The man knows her feelings but is determined to marry her. During the wedding ceremony, when the parson asks the usual question as to whether there is any impediment to the marriage, the woman says that there is: she loves a man other than her intended husband. But she is so set in her will that once she has decided to marry she intends to go through with it. Thus two inflexible wills are joined in a union that endures until the husband dies more than five years later.

A pettier stubbornness—or cussedness, as the country people would call it—is that of the husband in "Gentian," who hates all doctors and medicines. While he is suffering from a long and debilitating illness, his wife, unbeknown to him, gives him doses of gentian in his food, and as a result he regains his health. The wife, who is as conscientious as Martha Patch or Adoniram Dill, inadvisably tells him of her subterfuge. Next morning the wife cooks a good breakfast, but the husband has already been to the store and bought food which he proceeds to cook and eat, announcing, "I'm jest a-goin' to make sure I hev some tea, an' somethin' to eat without any gentian in it" (259). As he refuses to let his wife cook any of his meals in the future, she asks whether he would not prefer to have her go to her sister's house to live. He agrees that "mebbe 'twould be jest as well" (260), and so the two live apart until a return of the husband's illness breaks his will and he begs his wife to come back and doctor him.

"Gentian" has another dimension, as recent criticism has pointed out. It is one of Freeman's harsher treatments of marriage—in this case a marriage that "mocks male supremacy" and "dehumanizes" the female.[11] The husband's churlishness and his confidence that he can get his discarded wife back merely by beckoning clearly aroused in Freeman an indignation expressed by the simple statement of the situation. The submissiveness of the wife, who pathetically strives to do her "duty" as prescribed by custom and by Calvinist orthodoxy, obviously disturbed Freeman the most. Such appalling relationships of man and wife were not uncommon in back-country New England, as Robert Frost has recorded in such poems as "A Servant to Servants," "Home Burial," and "The Hill Wife."

Revolt

Sometimes the energies of the will in characters in the stories in *A Humble Romance* are directed into rebellion rather than into persistence in some whimsical course. In "A Tardy Thanksgiving" Mrs. Muzzy, a widow, decides that she has nothing to be thankful for and hence will spend Thanksgiving Day doing her "pig-work" (53)—preparing and packing the pork she has already had slaughtered. For a New England woman to ignore this most important of religious observances amounts to open revolt against family, neighbors, and God. She nevertheless persists, and her niece, Lizzie, who has been jilted by her beau, wishes to join her. But Mrs. Muzzy objects: "She had an inner consciousness, ever present to herself, that her state of mind was highly culpable, but she undertook the responsibility for herself with sullen defiance. It was another thing, however, to be responsible for a similar state in another" (55). The problem is resolved when Lizzie's beau returns, and Lizzie goes off with him much too readily to suit her aunt's sense of propriety. Thus Mrs. Muzzy sets about her pig-work alone. Her rebellion is soon put down, however, when she spills boiling water on her foot. The accident, she decides, has been a punishment from God; and having received this disciplining from the Deity, she is content to sit down to her turkey and plum pudding. The ending may seem somewhat contrived, but Mrs. Muzzy's initial rebelliousness seems realistic enough. Indeed, it has been suggested that the story may reflect Freeman's own state of mind after the deaths of her sister and both parents within a few years.[12]

Another story of rebellion is "A Moral Exigency," in which a minister's daughter, Eunice, refuses to marry a widower clergyman with four children, even though her refusal is extremely embarrassing to her father. Instead, she sets her cap at another girl's wealthy suitor and manages to win him for herself. Only when her rival is at the point of death from heartbreak does she relent, undergoing a change that resembles a conversion. Her "strong will broke down before the accusations of . . . conscience, which were so potent as to take upon themselves material shapes," for "all the familiar objects in [her] room . . . had a strange and awful look to her. Yet the change was in herself, not in them." (232).

In both these stories Freeman does not permit her women to sustain their revolts. Mrs. Muzzy's half-dormant conscience, awed by a supposed sign from God, returns her to the socially and religiously sanctioned view that one must be thankful even if there is nothing to be thankful for. Eunice at least perseveres in her refusal to let her father arrange her marriage—a somewhat daring stand for a daughter in her place and time. But her conscience causes her to return her lover to her friend. The distinction is a nice one. Freeman obviously thinks Eunice is right in defying her parent by declining to enter into a loveless marriage that promised only drudgery. But to betray another woman, whom she deeply loved, would be indefensible by more than merely conventional standards.

Moreover, there is a suggestion that Eunice has given up something more than her lover. Once, while "standing before her glass, . . . her fancy pictured to her, beside her own homely, sober face, another, a man's blond and handsome, with a gentle, almost womanish smile on the full red lips, and a dangerous softness in the blue eyes" (227). This imagined image is that of her lover, but its feminine characteristics suggest a merging, an identification with her own image in the mirror. It is plausible to surmise, as at least one critic has done, that in the mirror Eunice has seen two sides of herself—the more or less commonplace daughter of a parson living under the restrictions imposed on a woman by society and religion, and the latent aggressive, unconventional self that craves the liberty of action enjoyed by men such as her lover. For a time she gives rein to this second self in wresting her lover from her friend. Thus in her final relinquishing of her lover she was actually relinquishing a hitherto suppressed side of herself.[13] Perhaps in creating this mirror scene Freeman was recalling an occasion some years earlier when, out of "deviltry," she dressed as a man and was thrilled as she "gazed at her image in the mirror."[14]

Special Faculties

It is notable among the many headstrong villagers who appear in Freeman's fiction that some often act in accordance with their own whim or compulsion, usually to their detriment. But not always. At least two stories in *A Humble Romance* deal with characters who possess definite talents that they somehow find scope to exercise. In "Souvenirs" Nancy Weeks, a seamstress, has produced what passes in the village as an outstanding work of art. It is a wreath made of the hair of her relatives and ancestors, woven to resemble various flowers. Monstrosity spawned of sickly sentimentality though it is, it represents the apogee of the woman's creativity and has won her local renown.

On a different level is the mathematical talent of Mrs. Wilson Torry in "An Old Arithmetician." Mrs. Torry so loves to play with numbers that her highest pleasure, as she tells her parson, would be "to count up all the beautiful things in this creation. Just think of countin' all them red an' gold-colored leaves, an' all the grapes an' apples in the fall; and when it comes to the winter, all the flakes of snow, an' the sparkles of frost. . ." (370). So adept is she at "sums" that the minister and the schoolmaster bring her problems that they themselves cannot solve. She is proud of her "faculty," which she considers to be her one distinguishing mark; for she believes that every one, no matter how poor or uneducated, has been given some particular ability that sets him or her apart from all others—an idea akin to the Puritan belief that each person has been endowed by God with a special "calling" to follow in life.

"I ain't goin' to give it up yet"

Pride, whim, stubbornness, habit, sensitivity, indecision, rebelliousness, and monomania plague Freeman's characters. Sometimes these traits come into conflict with similar ones in others, sometimes with the consciences of the individuals themselves, sometimes with both. Resulting from such conflicts, a change of heart, a quasi-conversion, may occur as in the case of the husband in "Gentian" or the widow in "A Tardy Thanksgiving." Or there may be no change, as in "On the Walpole Road," "An Honest Soul," or "Old Lady Pingree"; in such stories stubbornness, pride, or "setness" prevails unabated. The most remarkable example of the latter in *A Humble Romance* is "A Patient Waiter," in which the main character, the spinster Fidelia Almy, refuses to admit that she has been jilted by her lover who left her forty years ago to seek in California the money that would enable them to get married but has not written her a single line since the day of his departure. Twice each day during all those years she has tramped the mile to the post office and back, even on Sundays when there is no mail, to pick up the letter that never comes. At home, she has refreshments ready for her momentarily expected lover. With her lives her niece, Lily Almy, who for a long time shares Fidelia's dream and believes in it. Later, when Fidelia is in her last illness, Lily herself makes the daily trips to the post office, though by now she knows that her aunt is insane and has been most of her life. There is nothing to do but to humor her as with her last breath she exhorts her niece to hurry for the mail: "He—promised he'd write, an' . . . *I ain't goin' to give it up yet*" (414).

Marjorie Pryse believes that this story "epitomizes the historical position of the late nineteenth-century New England woman."[15] More likely it is an extreme case of the plight of some women in a society that placed them at a disadvantage in achieving marriage and thus escaping the social stigma of spinsterhood. This, of course, is an aspect of the "awful pitifulness" (414) that is the theme of the story.

Confession and Repentance—and "What will folks say?"

The most impressive stories in *A Humble Romance* are those in which a change of heart does occur, and outstanding among these is "A Conquest of Humility." Lawrence Thayer fails to appear for his wedding with Delia Caldwell. All the couple's relatives—and these constitute most of the population of the village—have gathered at the bride's home. After a long wait Lawrence's father arrives to announce shamefacedly that his son refuses to come. The assumption is that he has fallen in love with pretty Olive Briggs, a saleswoman in a local store, and intends to marry her. Delia meets the situation by a brutal suppression of her feelings, her chief motivation being not to give way to her humiliation before the townspeople. She forces herself to walk among the guests and offers to return their gifts. She gets a schoolteaching job and resumes her former life. When she meets Lawrence, for whom she harbors a strong and angry contempt, she passes him without a look. At church she stares boldly at him and Olive. But there comes a day when Olive jilts Lawrence, and Delia has her revenge. "'I wonder how *he* feels,' she said to herself. She saw Lawrence Thayer, in her stead, in the midst of all that covert ridicule and obloquy, that galling sympathy, that agony of jealousy and betrayed trust. They distorted his face like flames; she saw him writhe through their liquid wavering" (429).

Lawrence is in fact jeered at by his mates, but "he went about doggedly. He was strong in silence . . ." (429). Delia and Lawrence could easily have perpetuated their stubborn, silent hate through the remainder of their lives—as so often happens with characters in Freeman's stories. Their humiliation and resentment could be buried under taciturnity, which would harden their spirits to granite. The only hope for a renewal of their lives is for one of them to make a step from humiliation with its exaggerated pride and bitterness to humility with its restoration of spiritual tranquility. This at least was the way taught by the Calvinistic and Puritan New England church. First must come confession of the wrongness of one's hate; next, repentance.

At any rate, the deadlock between Delia and Lawrence, who retain a deeply submerged but substantial remnant of their original love for each other, is resolved by Lawrence's total subduing of his pride. On the second anniversary of the day on which he jilted Delia he asks the former wedding guests to assemble at her home. He admits his guilt, begs Delia's forgiveness, and asks her to marry him. Her answer is: "'I never will'. . . . [Her] whole nature had been set to these words; they had to be spoken" (435). Yet she understands the sincerity of his offer. He is clearly repentant; he had not rigged this scene as a clever device to win her back now that he had lost Olive. Furthermore, Delia may have recognized something of herself in him, much as the heroine of "A Moral Exigency" seemed to recognize something of herself in her lover; for Lawrence was a "shy young man" with "a sweet womanish face" (429–30). "'A coward and mean.' Yes, he had been, but—Yes, there was some excuse for him—there was. Is not every fault wedded to its own excuse, that pity may be born into the world?" (435–36).

Lawrence is not surprised by the refusal. He knows her "enduring will, her power of indignation" (436). He turns to leave. "There was a certain dignity about him. He had in reality pulled himself up to the level of his own noble, avowed sentiments" (436). Delia gazes after him relentlessly. A girl begins to cry. Delia glances at one of Lawrence's relatives. What she sees makes her spring forward. "'You needn't look at him in that way,' she cries out. 'I'm going to marry him. Lawrence, come back'" (436).

What had Delia seen in the woman's eyes that made her so suddenly reverse herself? A moment before, Delia had observed, as if in a triumphant dream, all the Thayers and Caldwells sitting there; and she had thought how they would talk and laugh at Lawrence for his failure. In Mrs. Erastus Thayer's glance Delia had detected the beginning of that ridicule, which would be a perpetual crucifixion for its victim.

Fully to understand "A Conquest of Humility" and many other of Freeman's stories, one must review the conditions of village life in New England during her lifetime. In some ways there had been little change since colonial days. Freeman's villages are isolated, somewhat self-containing communities, swallowed up in a vast geography much as were the seventeenth-century settlements. Everyone knows everyone else; one can be sure that one's every action will be scrutinized and commented on according to the code of behavior sanctioned by the local church. One is born into a family whose annual income has been continuously assessed by the villagers with a view to classifying it as poor—a matter of shame—or well-to-do—a matter of satisfaction. On Sabbaths the child attends church perhaps as many as three times; any particular laxity on the part of the parents arouses strong public disapprobation. Constantly one's conduct is referred to the single standard: "What will folks say?" If a boy enters a general store and his presence brings a hush upon the bystanders, the boy knows at once that his family was being talked about and has had adverse judgment passed on it. But at any event his clothes will be peered at for signs of poverty; his face for signs of illness. And the findings, whatever they are, will contribute toward the villagers' estimate of the family's material and spiritual status. The child's own conduct, too, will be examined and judged.

When a boy or girl approaches adulthood, attraction to the opposite sex begins. Two young people walk home from church together several mornings. A young man calls a few times at a young woman's house on Sunday evenings, and the two sit in the mildew-smelling parlor. Such is courtship in nineteenth-century New England. The rest of the town will, of course, have observed these proceedings, and soon it will pronounce the couple engaged. Marriage may take place soon or at any time within the next ten, twenty, or thirty years. If the relationship is broken off, the one responsible for the break will be subjected to condemnation and the jilted to ridicule.

What Delia sees, then, in the eyes of the village gossip, Mrs. Erastus Thayer, is a glimmering of the hell of public mockery and revilement that awaits Lawrence once he passes through her doors jilted and a jilter. Her vision moves her to compassion, and her sense of justice is repelled by the disproportionate fury of Lawrence's punishment at the hands of the townspeople. Knowing from personal experience the agony he will suffer, she does the one thing that will save him; she accepts his offer of marriage. His bloodthirsty tormentors are at once appeased.

"An Old House and an Old Woman"

According to Willa Cather, Sarah Orne Jewett once made the remark that when "an old house and an old woman came together in her brain with a click, she knew a story was under way."[16] Apparently Freeman's brain clicked in the same way. Hers is a woman's world, especially in the earlier stories. As one critic facetiously put it, "In the census of a Mary Wilkins Freeman village the proportions of inhabitants would approximate sixty women upwards of seventy years old, five old men, fifteen middle-aged women, eight middle-aged men, seven girls, three eligible bachelors, two children."[17] The setting for most of her stories, if dramatized, would be very simple; nine tenths of the action takes place in a kitchen, the other tenth in the best parlor. Out-of-doors nature is seen and appreciated, but from the kitchen window or on a walk to the village store to replenish the kitchen supplies. The grander aspects of nature—mountains, lakes, the ocean—are almost entirely lacking.

Among the New England peasantry—and as one reads Freeman's work one realizes there is such a peasantry, with all the virtues and vices of the species—the women do not usually work in the fields and in the stables, both of which are the exclusive domain of the menfolk. The division of the spheres of activity are very sharp. On a New England farm of a generation or two ago, a farmer's wife might go for years without even entering the barn. The farmhouse is the woman's realm and one which Freeman knew well because of her intimacy with the Wales family in Randolph. Cooking, sewing, the amassing of trousseaux, the care of house pets (especially cats) and children, and the cultivation of flowers are the activities that occupy the farm or village woman. Thus Freeman's stories are rich in the description of interiors as vivid as those in Mark Twain's books. The kitchen with its hearth or stove; the best parlor, smelling of unheated gentility, with its knick-knacks, Bible, photograph albums, and horsehair sofa; the bare wooden furnishings of the bedchambers; and perhaps the dooryard with its hollyhocks and shade trees—these she presents with a loving care and an accuracy that give her stories value as social history.

If Freeman's world is a woman's world, it also is a world largely of single women—another reflection of real-life conditions. The Civil War and the westward migrations had decreased the number of men. Freeman's young women and girls have one main goal in life as a general rule—to find a husband in a scarce market. So intense is their purpose that when it is thwarted the resultant stresses are the stuff of drama. Nor do the women submit easily to defeat; the case of Fidelia Almy, who nursed her hope for forty years, is not untypical of a Freeman story. This is not to say that Freeman shared the view, so embedded in the popular mores, that a young woman's main goal in life should be marriage. There is ample evidence of her ambivalence on the subject.

An old woman in an old house is, indeed, for Freeman as for Jewett, a typical situation. But in the Freeman story, unlike the Jewett one, the old woman will be undergoing some sort of spiritual crisis—a rebellion, a wrestling with her conscience, an unprecedented exertion of the will. Sometimes in the case of an old single woman, a marriage takes place, but the story has essentially dealt with her spinsterhood. A story that might be called archetypal in *A Humble Romance* and in Freeman's later work is "An Object of Love," which Jewett, incidentally, found to be a model of short fiction. The elderly Ann Millett lives alone with her cat in a "tiny, white-painted house, with a door and one window in front, and a little piazza, over which the roof jutted, and on which the kitchen door opened, on the rear corner" (266). As the story begins, Ann Millet is taking in her squash because of the possibility of frost. She is resigned, on the surface, to her lot: "I'd orter be thankful. I've got my Bible an' Willy [the cat], an' a roof over my head, an' enough to eat an' wear; an' a good many folks hev to be alone, as fur as other other folks is concerned, on this airth. An' p'rhaps some other woman ain't lonesome because I am, an' maybe she'd be one of the kind that didn't like cats, an' wouldn't hev got along half as well as me. No: I've got a good many mercies to be thankful fur—more'n I deserve. I never orter complain" (268).

So Ann Millett has made herself a life keeping house for her cat, attending church with unbroken regularity, and assuring herself twenty times a day that she "orter be thankful." But, were she really thankful, she would not have reminded herself so often. Revolt against what she considered God's predestined plan for her life is latent within her. And revolt erupts one night when she comes from prayer meeting to find that Willy has disappeared and is not to be found after a search of several days. In "A Tardy Thanksgiving" a widow refuses to thank the God who has taken her husband from her; and Ann Millet, in full rebellion for the first time in her life, refuses to attend church to worship a God who has deprived her of all companionship except that of a cat and now has taken even it. "Ann Millet, in spite of all excuses that could be made for her, was for the time a wicked, rebellious old woman. And she was as truly so as if this petty occasion for it had been a graver one in other peoples' estimation" (276).

The minister, dull country parson that he is, expostulates heavy-handedly with her. Neighbor children offer other cats. But Ann Millet is iron-willed. She has "a nature that could rally an enormous amount of strength for persistency" (277). When she finally returns to a meeting, the parson rejoices. "The cat has come back," she says (279). The cat, indeed, had been locked in her cellar where it had been meowing, unheard by the somewhat deaf woman, until a neighbor had detected its presence. Ann had let the cat into the cellar before going to prayer meeting and on returning had forgotten that she had done so.

As in much of Freeman's fiction, there is a rather bitter humor in this story. But underlying it is a most serious substratum. Had Ann Millet subconsciously resented the cat which had been a substitute in life for husband and children? Freeman does not answer the question—or ask it, for that matter. But beyond doubt she expects the reader to ask it and to answer it affirmatively. Freeman had a personal knowledge about single women and their cats. When she was left without parents or a sister to live alone in Brattleboro and Randolph, she, too, cherished a cat and experienced distress when it disappeared. She was deeply interested in the relationships between human beings and animals—as we shall see later—and these relationships were by no means ones solely of affection, nor were they free of resentment or other negative emotions.

"Like the best modern work everywhere"

Any reader of Freeman's story collections soon becomes aware that she combines in her fiction humor with tragedy and pathos. In summaries of the stories, the humor may not be apparent, and in certain stories it undoubtedly is nonexistent. But Martha Patch's sewing and resewing her quilts in order to get one rag in its rightful place, the two old paupers superciliously criticizing the gifts that keep them alive, Adoniram Dill feeling he is unwanted because he is censured for chasing a butterfly, Fidelia Almy visiting the post office twice a day for forty years, though she has not received a single letter in all that time—those foibles elicit at least a subdued laughter as well as tears.

Freeman at times injects humor into an otherwise serious situation by the device of understatement, which in turn is characteristic of New

England speech. When the wife in "Gentian" suggests that she might as well leave her husband since he will not let her cook for him, he laconically answers, "Mebbe 'twould be jest as well" (260). The calmness of the phrasing is so inappropriate to the gravity of the step being taken—the breakup of a marriage of most of a lifetime—that the reader cannot restrain a smile. Yet a passionate tirade on the part of either the wife or the husband would have been disastrous to the story. The husband's tone is just right, not only because it is exactly what he would have said as a New England countryman but also because it saves by irony what otherwise would be bathos or melodrama. Unconscious irony on the part of the character involved also lends humor to "In Butterfly Time." Adoniram, having broken his engagement forty years ago because of his fiancée's mother's slighting remarks, finally learns that no offense had been intended. Adoniram's mother then asks if he is going right over to see his sweetheart and make it up with her. "I guess not tonight, mother," he answers. And she says, "Well, mebbe *'tis* jest as well to wait till to-morrer. I don't want Mis' Wheat to think you was in too much of a rush" (326).

Everywhere Freeman shows herself adept at capturing the understatement, the irony, the cautiousness of New England rural speech, a fact that becomes painfully evident when, in later books, she has Virginians and others speaking in Yankee cadences. But in her New England stories the effect is just right, and she makes liberal use of dialogue to carry as much of her action as possible. Nor does she make the mistake of so many local-color writers who attempt a phonetic transcription of dialect. She uses misspellings charily, just enough to indicate the flavor of the language she records. Her Vermonters and her Massachusetts people speak alike, which is linguistically not quite accurate, though the two areas are roughly in the same dialect region. She makes no claims like Mark Twain's to the effect that he employed five varieties of Missouri patois in *Huckleberry Finn*. Rhythmically New England speech tends to be the same throughout the six states; and these rhythms, which she doubtless produced without effort from her own speech patterns, provide the distinguishing marks of her dialogue—as well as of her narrative and exposition.

In an age when literary style, under the guidance of Twain, Jewett, and Howells, was abandoning rhetoric and verbosity for directness and simplicity, Freeman's writing was very modern. Her style anticipates the concreteness and straightforwardness of such authors as Sherwood Anderson, Hemingway, and the Gertrude Stein of *Three Lives*. Image-making words of Anglo-Saxon origin, simple or compound sentences, but few complex ones, and repetition of key words and phrases characterize her early writing. The opening paragraph of "An Old Arithmetician," which is typical, comes directly to the point; it appeals to several of the senses; it is as uncomplicated as a primer; it contains only one figure of speech, and that an unobtrusive one. Indeed, it could have been written by Anderson, Stein, or Hemingway:

A strong, soft south wind had been blowing the day before, and the trees had dropped nearly all their leaves. There were left only a few brownish-golden ones dangling on the elms and hardly any at all on the maples. There were many trees on the street, and the fallen leaves were heaped high. Mrs. Wilson Torry's little door-yard was ankle-deep with them. The air was full of their odor, which could affect the spirit like a song, and mingled with it was the scent of grapes. (368)

It has been said that Freeman wrote simply because she was incapable of a more involved style. Later, to be sure, she attempted a more rhetorical manner, with disastrous results. Later still she advised would-be authors to write clearly and simply.[18] In her early writing she was quite likely influenced, perhaps unconsciously, by the Bible, which is also concrete in diction and uncomplex in sentence structure. She may also have been impressed by the naturalness of her fellow New England writer, Sarah Orne Jewett. But the direct influence of New England conversational style, itself resonant with biblical echoings, should not be overlooked. Her biographer, Edward Foster, surmises that much of her material came from stories told by countrywomen— dressmakers, relatives, and friends in and around Brattleboro and Randolph. Some of the tales of these gossips would be told so frequently that they would have acquired an economy of diction and a dramatic quality even in their oral form. Needless to say, they would be lacking in the adornments of "literary" writing. "On the Walpole Road," in fact, is told in the form of a gossip session between two women riding in a buggy along a country road. They speak first of the threatening weather and then of their horse, and finally they drift into a story of local interest. Most of Freeman's stories lack this sort of framework; but their content is of the stuff that gossip thrives on; though pruned of most of the digression common to gossip, they are told in the colloquial language of the New England village, with the earthy irony typical of that speech.

Writing in "The Editor's Study" in *Harper's New Monthly* for September 1887, William Dean Howells voiced praise that was typical of the reception of Freeman's work. The stories in *A Humble Romance,* he wrote, "are good enough through and through, and whoever loves the face of common humanity will find pleasure in them. They are peculiarly American, and they are peculiarly 'narrow' in a certain way, and yet they are like the best modern work everywhere in their directness and simplicity."[19] He compares them to Turgenev's and Björnson's work in their lack of rhetorical flourishings. Such writing he considers to be typical of the times. One author does not copy it from another. Though Howells finds that some of the stories in *A Humble Romance* suffer from sentimentality, he does not consider this a ruinous defect. As a group, he thinks they are a complete representation of New England village and farm life. The best of her work he compares favorably with Jewett's.

Chapter Three

A New England Nun
and Other Stories

By 1891 Freeman had published enough additional stories, mainly in the Harper periodicals, to make another collection. *A New England Nun and Other Stories,* as the volume was titled, contains a half dozen or so pieces that rank with her very best, as well as a number of second- or third-rate quality. Its heights of excellence and its depths of medi- ocrity exceed those of *A Humble Romance,* which maintained a more constantly high level. *A New England Nun* treats no important themes not represented in the earlier collection, but it emphasizes some, like that of revolt, by more frequent treatment.

Studies in Passivity

As a student of the will, Freeman in *A Humble Romance* had presented cases in varying degrees of nearly total atrophy or passivity of volition. Such stories were "A Symphony in Lavender" and "A Lover of Flowers," the latter dealing with a young man who substitutes a love of flowers for the love of a woman. The title story of *A New England Nun* records a similar case but with greater literary skill. Louisa Ellis and Joe Dag- get have been engaged for fifteen years. Joe has been in Australia most of the time, earning money for his marriage. Louisa has remained in her sleepy New England village—her parents have died in the mean- while—where she falls into a routine of sewing, of caring for her sup- posedly vicious dog Caesar, of keeping her house spotlessly clean, and, in short, of speeding the process of becoming a spinster. When Joe returns, the two proceed with their wedding plans, but both realize soon—without confessing it to each other—that they are no longer in love. She is loath to change her comfortable routine, and he has become strongly attracted to Lily Dyer, a pretty and passionate girl working for his mother. In this story, every one is too considerate, too self- sacrificing. Rather than hurt one another's feelings, all three principals scrupulously honor the fifteen-year-old engagement. To preserve its sanctity, three lives seem doomed to misery. But one evening, while she is taking a stroll, Louisa overhears Lily and Joe talking on the road. They are speaking of their love. They deplore their treachery to Louisa and decide to desist from it. Lily will go away; Joe will go through with the marriage. The next evening, when Joe comes to call, Louisa, prompted mainly by reluctance to change her way of life, releases him from their engagement. Neither of the two mentions Lily, who is actually not much of a consideration in Louisa's decision. Joe and Lily, the reader assumes, soon marry. "Louisa, all alone by herself that night, wept a little, she hardly knew why; but the next morning, on waking, she felt like a queen who, after fearing lest her domain be wrested away from her, sees it finally insured in her possession. . . . If Louisa Ellis had sold her birthright she did not know it, the taste of the potage was so delicious, and had been her sole satisfaction for so long. Serenity and placid narrowness had become to her as the birthright itself."[1]

The only didactic sentence in the story is the last one just quoted, and it does not constitute a discordance. It was not needed, however. With its evocation of the torpid, dusty summertime atmosphere of a remote New England village and with its description of Louisa's manner of living (symbolized by the canary singing in its cage) and with the merging of the environment and all its exacting pettiness with Louisa's character, this is well nigh a perfect story—one worthy of standing with the best of Katherine Mansfield or Anton Chekhov.

What has happened to Louisa is abundantly clear without the one-sentence statement of it that the author, like Hawthorne, feels compelled to make. Like certain of Henry James's characters Louisa has done no less than permit herself to become unfitted for the life that, rightly or wrongly, society and, apparently, she at one time, considered "normal" for a woman. What has happened to her is adroitly symbolized not only by the canary but by her chief pastime, that of distilling the essences of rose petals in a little apparatus she owns and storing the oils away in vials for no foreseeable use. What would be the status with her of any man whom she might marry, were she not wise enough to steer clear of marriage altogether, is suggested by the fate of Caesar, the luckless dog which has spent fourteen years on a chain because in puppyhood he bit a neighbor. In a letter to Mary Louise Booth, her editor at *Harper's Bazar,* Freeman told of a dog chained thirteen years because of an offense similar to Caesar's.[2] Freeman, always fond of animals, expressed shock at this treatment of the dog. But in the story, in dealing with Caesar, she employs sarcastic humor. Having earned a reputation for viciousness, Caesar has never known the joy of barking at a woodchuck or of finding and burying a bone. Nothing that belongs to Louisa may have contact with the more earthy aspects of life. Next to Joe's tracking dust onto her immaculate carpets and disarranging the books on the parlor table, his avowal that he is someday going to unchain Caesar strikes the most terror into her heart. And perhaps Caesar's present bondage arouses misgivings in Joe as to his future if he marries Louisa.

When Louisa releases Joe, she opts for a prolongment of her "nun's" life that only death will terminate. But she also redeems herself to a degree. Unwilling to break out of her cage, she at least comes to terms with herself. Not only does her decision partly interrupt the unrippled flow of years of passivity, but it marks her as possessing a sense of moral realism, which Howells (in *The Rise of Silas Lapham,* for instance) repeatedly declared is an ingredient of literary realism. To force herself to go through with the marriage, knowing as she does that the honorable Joe stands ready, would make three people miserable; the result would be a threefold self-sacrifice and nothing more, and hence would be an immoral act sanctioned only by a mawkish sentimentality. When Howells referred to Freeman's realism, it was as much to her sense of moral rightness—as opposed to sentimental rightness—as to her accurate depiction of rural life.

It would be wrong, however, to dismiss Louisa's way of life as entirely trivial and unfulfilling, though her fellow villagers and contemporary readers would doubtless have considered them so. Instead of marriage she has deliberately chosen an alternative in which her sewing and her meticulous housekeeping—themselves forms of artistic expression—provide her very real satisfaction.[3] The suggestion offers itself whether Freeman, unmarried at the age of forty when she wrote the story and hesitant to the last about her eventual marriage ten years later, may have put some of herself into her fictional "nun." Some contemporaries, among them Hamlin Garland, saw a resemblance, at least in her way of life.[4] It is especially tempting to equate Louisa's distillation of rose petals with Freeman's distillation of life into her stories; and contemporary descriptions of her—for example, "she was as fine & dainty as old point lace or Chinese porcelain"[5]—evoke an image of Louisa Ellis.

Freeman's prose style and ability to create mood are nowhere employed more effectively than in "A New England Nun," as may be seen in the first paragraph of the story:

It was late in the afternoon, and the light was waning. There was a difference in the look of the tree shadows out in the yard. Somewhere in the distance cows were lowing and a little bell was tinkling; now and then a farm-wagon tilted by, and the dust flew; some blue-shirted laborers with shovels over their shoulders plodded past; little swarms of flies were dancing up and down before peoples' faces in the soft air. There seemed to be a gentle stir arising from everywhere for the mere sake of subsidence—a very premonition of rest and hush and night. (1)

In evoking the peaceful atmosphere of this village scene, Freeman makes use of images, all of them subdued, that appeal to the senses of sight, hearing, and feeling ("the soft air"); and the slow movement of the plodding laborers and the wagon that tilted (i.e., swayed unsteadily) along enhance the effect. It has been pointed out that in this paragraph Freeman consciously or unconsciously echoes the first two stanzas of Thomas Gray's "Elegy Written in a Country Churchyard,"[6] a poem familiar to most people in Freeman's day and ours:

> The Curfew tolls the knell of parting day,
> The lowing herd winds slowly o'er the lea,
> The ploughman homeward plods his weary way,
> And leaves the world to darkness and to me.
>
> Now fades the glimmering landscape on the sight,
> And all the air a solemn stillness holds,
> Save where the beetle wheels his droning flight,
> And drowsy tinklings lull the distant folds.[7]

The resemblances of Gray's verse to Freeman's description are obvious, and each is intended to suggest to the reader the aura of tranquility of a country village and the quiet dignity of the villagers.

But Freeman's description serves also as a prelude to the next several paragraphs, in which she shifts the scene from the outdoors to the interior of Louisa's house, where the same serenity exists. Outside and inside, peace and security reign, and peace and security are what Louisa has come to value above all else, so that to retain them she readily relinquishes marriage and the turbulence and change it might bring into her life.

Settings like that in "A New England Nun" are typical of most of Freeman's village stories. Even where the action of the narrative is less sedate, as in "A Village Singer," the village with its uneventful, usually calm routine is present in the background, and it is in this tranquil atmosphere—for example, in "A Church Mouse"—that conflicts and misunderstandings are resolved. In writing of villages Freeman is writing of an environment in which she was born and grew up and did her work until she was fifty—and Metuchen, New Jersey, where she later lived, had much the same village atmosphere.

Two other stories of passivity in *A New England Nun* are "A Village Lear" and "Sister Liddy." The latter—one of the most powerful of all of Freeman's tales—exudes a mood of utter despair and futility and completely lacks the humor, sentiment, or pathos characteristic of so many of her stories. In the town poorhouse, which also serves as a madhouse, the sane and insane poor share an unrelieved wretchedness. The time is late autumn, when chilly rains slant across fields of stubble. The house itself is a barracks with long empty corridors and bleak common rooms through which mingle the laughter of playing children, the shrieks of the demented, the moans of the sick, and the sighs of the paupers. Most notable among the inmates are a tall insane woman who predicts the imminent end of the world; a fat old woman with no brain to be demented, who amuses herself with vicious gossip and spiteful comments about her fellows; a pretty old woman who finds solace in her long-past reputation as a belle; Polly Moss, a pitiable pauper, who has had nothing in her life worth remembering but is kind-hearted and amuses herself and the children by playing ball with them; Sally, who spends her days tearing her bedding to shreds; a young woman, sick and melancholy and abandoned; and the impassive matron, Mrs. Arms, who presides over this inferno as stolidly as if it were a chicken coop full of placidly clucking hens.

There is no plot to speak of. The inmates wander on and off the stage like the people in Maxim Gorky's *Lower Depths,* which in no way surpasses Freeman's story as a "naturalistic" study of the despair arising from social degeneration. Sometimes one of the insane erupts into violence, but in general the dreary routine goes on uninterrupted.

The title of the story derives from Polly Moss's invention of a beautiful sister, Liddy, to combat the boastings of the other women as they recall their past lives. Polly has had no past any more than she has had a sister, but her stories of her imagined sister put to shame anything the others can conjure up from the drab desolation of their lives. Sister Liddy sang like an angel, dressed like a princess, was married to a fabulously wealthy man, and lived in Boston. Polly's story, one critic thinks, is a parody of the sentimentality current in the fiction of the time (and occasionally present in Freeman's writings).[8] Polly's listeners half believe her, perhaps because it is less boring to believe than disbelieve. But Polly, among her other miseries, suffers from a New England conscience; and two weeks later, while dying of pneumonia, she reveals her deceit to a group at her bedside. With her confession the story closes, lacking the "happy ending" that fashion and her editors induced Freeman to impose on her fiction more often than not. To be sure, as Polly is dying, the melancholy, lonesome young woman ecstatically rushes in to announce that her lover has come to take her away. But this unexpected good fortune, if it is that, only intensifies the hopelessness of those who remain.

Ann Douglas Wood, who thinks "Sister Liddy" is "one of the most powerful stories written in America," describes it as "a spectrum of obsolete and frustrated womanhood."[9] The comment is perceptive; but another critic, Marjorie Pryse, has called rural New England "a world transformed into a quasimatriarchal one."[10] Assuming that Wood takes "Sister Liddy" as allegorizing the plight of women in New England, we are confronted with a seeming contradiction between her statement and Pryse's. Yet the paradox can be explained. Because of the loss of men in the Civil War and the flight of many others to the manufacturing cities and to the West, women outnumbered men in the region, with the result that many women who wished to marry were unable to find a husband. Since custom and tradition regarded marriage as indispensable for a woman's social and personal fulfillment, unmarried women—with the exception of a few, like Louisa Ellis, who had found satisfying alternatives—would feel frustrated. Furthermore, though numerically in the majority, women were excluded from voting and from holding political offices, nor were they permitted to vote in church matters, even though as a group they were the most faithful churchgoers. Perhaps these exclusions, so embedded in the accepted and age-old way of life, did not rankle most women—they seem not to have done so with Freeman herself. More frustrating would be the exclusion from gainful employment, both because of the region's serious economic depression and the limitation on the kind of jobs considered suitable for women (for example, schoolteaching). Thus much of Freeman's earlier fiction explores the way women marooned in the remote and impoverished rural villages of New England coped with these deprivations.

Freeman, of course, did not people her stories solely with spinsters. But more often than not, the marriages she depicts are also frustrating to one or both of the partners; and, as has been seen, some women, as in "A Symphony in Lavender," "A Taste of Honey," and "A New England Nun," avoid marriage consciously and, within the general impoverishment of village life, fashion existences that are satisfying to them. Others, like Martha Patch in "An Honest Soul," struggle desperately against destitution; and a few, as in "Sister Liddy," have been defeated and live, if at all, on dreams and hallucinations. It is true, furthermore, as Kipling observed in describing conditions in Vermont in the 1890s, that some men, having been dominated by strong-willed women, particularly in their schooling, and through their childhood and adolescence, developed a lifelong fear of the opposite sex.[11] A number of Freeman's writings—for example, *Pembroke*—substantiate Kipling's observations.

The Opening of the Floodgates

One way in which some of the women in Freeman's stories coped was by outright, sometimes spectacular revolt, after years of frustration or oppression. Two of her best-known tales, both in *A New England Nun*, are records of such revolts. The first, and the better written of the two, is "A Village Singer," Candace Whitcomb, the leading soprano in the village choir for forty years, is dismissed because her voice has begun to crack. In her place a younger woman is hired. Candace is informed of her dismissal at a surprise party, at which she is given a photograph album. The next Sabbath, when the new soprano, Alma Way, sings a solo, Candace shrills out with a different hymn from her house next door to the church. The weather is hot and the windows of both buildings are open; so the interference is fully effective. Mr. Pollard, the minister, later calls on the old singer and expostulates with her, but she repulses him with defiance and fury. What has enraged Candace is the manner in which she has been let go. "If they'd turned me right out fair an' square," she says, "showed me the door, an' said, 'Here, you get out,' but to go an' spill molasses, as it were, all over the threshold, tryin' to make me think it's all nice and sweet—." Not knowing to whom to return the album, she uses it as a footrest as she harangues the parson, who is "aghast and bewildered at this outbreak" (27–28).

Freeman describes Candace's emotions as "tropical, and more than tropical, for a New England nature has a floodgate, and the power it releases is an accumulation. Candace Whitcomb had been a quiet woman, so delicately resolute that the quality had been scarcely noticed in her, and her ambition had been unsuspected. Now the resolution and the ambition appeared raging over her whole self. . . . To this obscure woman, kept relentlessly by circumstance in a narrow track, singing in the village choir had been as much as Italy was to Napoleon—and now on her island of exile she was still showing fight" (28–30).

Candace spoils the afternoon church-meeting as effectively as she did the morning one. Her nephew, who is engaged to Alma Way, tries to reason with her, but she responds by threatening to disinherit him. That evening before going to bed she looks out and sees the red glow of a forest fire in the distance. Within herself is "the roar of an intenser fire" (33). She lies awake all night, and in the morning she is ill, consumed by the previous day's emotional conflagration. She never rises again. But she has softened enough to apologize to the minister, to assure her nephew that his inheritance is safe, and to ask Alma to sing for her. The ending may smack of the sentimental, but the sentimentality is an expression of the characters rather than of the author. After the single emotional eruption of a lifetime, Candace would inevitably return to the personal and social norm. Even the photograph album, a symbol of extreme sentimentality, would be bearable.

But Candace has not suffered defeat. She has met head-on two deep-seated prejudices. She has been dismissed, she has told the minister, because of her age and because she is a woman. Her voice may not be as pure as when she was young, but it is still strong, and her younger replacement is not so much her superior. The minister himself is old, she tells him, and there has been no move to replace him, though his sermons may not be so brilliant as they once were. Furthermore, the choir master, who is her age and over the years has been her admirer in the indecisive way common to suitors in Freeman's fiction, has not been let go. In short, Candace makes it clear that as an elderly woman she has been treated unjustly.[12] Having made clear her awareness of what has been done to her, she does revert to the village norm, as do the protagonists in "A Tardy Thanksgiving" and "A Conflict Ended." The eruption that has convulsed the hitherto unruffled surface of an obscure and restricted life cannot be sustained in full force to the end. But she has had her day and has made a point that the villagers (and Freeman's readers) will not soon forget. Nor has Candace's indignation totally vanished. On her deathbed she asks Alma to sing to her the hymn "Jesus, Lover of My Soul." When the girl has finished, Candace's remark is: "You flatted a little on—soul" (36).

A less violent but more successful eruption of surface passivity into rebellion is that of the farmwife Sarah Penn in "The Revolt of Mother," Freeman's most widely acclaimed story during her lifetime and after. In it are combined the themes of rebellion and of the suddenly redirected will. Adoniram Penn is as unyielding a New England farmer as any of those who populate Freeman's pages. For years he has postponed the building of the new house he had promised his wife to replace their present one, which "was scarcely as commodious for people as the little boxes under the barn eaves were for doves" (449–50), But when he builds a new barn instead of the house, he goes too far. While he is away for a week buying a horse, Sarah moves her family into the new barn and sets up housekeeping there, an act that thrills the village gossips and shatters her husband's will when he returns. Reduced to tears, Adoniram consents to cut the windows and put up the partitions that will convert the barn into a comfortable dwelling.

In this story there is more humor and less intensity than in "A Village Singer." In fact, its main intention was probably comic. Freeman in later years was critical of the story, asserting that in it she had had sacrificed the truth—had, indeed, told a "big fib."[13] No woman with the courage or imagination of Sarah Penn, she said, ever existed in New England. A true New England woman of the period would have concurred with her husband in deferring her own comfort to that of the farm animals, on which the family's livelihood depended. Yet Freeman's fiction constantly belies this assertion. It abounds in strong-minded women capable of withering the most formidable "cussedness" in their menfolk, and by no means all of these women are materialists who would sacrifice the well-being of their families to the greater productivity of the farm. To many of them, flowers or some other objects of beauty, some human relationship—above all, their own integrity and sense of worth—may be much more important than money or possessions. While the actual occurrences in "The Revolt of Mother" may be outside the realm of possibility, the spirit behind them is true to life, especially if allowance is made for the individualism latent in New England village character, male or female. At any rate, the story caught the imagination of the reading public and took on a significance that might have surprised Freeman. For example, it is reported that Theodore Roosevelt, while governor of New York, recommended to a group of mothers whom he was addressing that they read "The Revolt of Mother" for its moral lesson.[14] From then on, if not earlier, the story

was by many regarded as a serious tract on women's rights—which is
perhaps too heavy a burden for it to carry.

Yet it is true that Sarah remarks to her daughter, who also hopes to
have a new house: "You ain't found out yet we're women-folks, Nanny
Penn. . . . You ain't seen enough of men-folks yet to. One of these
days you'll find it out, an' then you'll know that we know only what
men-folks think we do . . . an' how we'd ought to reckon men-folks
in with Providence, an' not complain of what they do any more than
we do of the weather" (451–52). Actually, Sarah does not subscribe to
this belief, for when a real need arises she talks "plain" (455) to Adoniram and, more importantly, she *acts*. Her motivation is clear. First,
she is a skilled housekeeper and she needs a house worth the exertion
of her skill. Second, her house is inferior to those of other villagers,
even those of poor families. Last, and decisively, her daughter deserves
a decent house in which to entertain her friends and receive her suitors
and eventually be married. Once Sarah Penn moves into the barn, despite the expostulations of the minister, and reduces her husband to
tears of remorse, she reverts to her role as willing wife and housekeeper.
Yet she has "revolted" in a just cause and has had her way, and one can
be sure that in the future Adoniram will be a bit less high-handed.
However, the story is a good-natured one, carrying the theme, of
course, that in New England, at least, women need not always submit
to their husbands' unreasonable demands. There is exhilaration in
seeing Adoniram put down. Yet it is interesting that Freeman herself,
refusing to sign a petition in 1899 by women against the war in the
Philippines, wrote: "I always am keenly alive to the futility of all feminine flights in the face of masculine powers that be (always makes me
think of hens) but I don't want all those women to think I am a
fighter."[15]

Self-laceration

Behind the eccentric stubbornness of some of her characters Freeman
saw an impulse of self-punishment, or self-laceration, arising out of
hurt pride and humiliation (as distinct from humility). The spectacle
of human perversity, or irrational, self-destructive action, fascinated
her as it did Dostoyevski and Poe, both of whom, incidentally, she had
read, and in a number of her writings she probes for the motivation of
such irrationality. Thus in "A Poetess" (in *A New England Nun*) a spin-

ster of fifty, who grows flowers rather than the vegetables she needs for her very sustenance, has won a place for herself in the village as a writer of poetry, the sentimental quality of which is symbolized by the chirpings of a canary that she keeps as her companion in song. One day a bereaved friend asks her to write a poem commemorating her dead baby. The poetess complies with her mawkish best, and the admiring friend has copies printed and sends them to all her neighbors and relatives. Unfortunately, a copy gets into the hands of the minister, who himself has literary pretensions as well as some discrimination. A gossiping neighbor soon triumphantly reports to the poetess that the parson considers her poem to be trash and the distribution of copies of it to be in extremely bad taste. As she listens, the poetess's face becomes "like a pale wedge of ice between her curls" (153). When her gossiping neighbor leaves, the poetess gathers all her poems, burns them, and deposits the ashes in a teapot. But first she vents her feelings to God concerning his dispensation of things: "I'd like to know if you think it's fair. Had I ought to have been born with the wantin' to write poetry if I couldn't write it—had I? Had I ought to have been let to write all my life, an' not know before there wa'n't any use in it? Would it be fair if that canary-bird there, that ain' never done anything but sing, should turn out not to be singin'?" (154–55).

The poetess's notion about her relationship with God is peculiarly legalistic. It is reminiscent of the old Puritan federal theology, according to which God almost literally enters into legally binding covenants with his elect. Thus if one is a fully converted church member, one may assume that one is of the elect with all the immunities and privileges pertaining to that estate and that one comes under the covenant of grace, which guarantees salvation through Christ. God and his elect are under contract to one another.

The poetess is a devout church member, and though the federal or covenant theology is long since dead, enough of its spirit lingers to make her feel resentful at what seems a trick played on her by God. "A Tardy Thanksgiving" and "An Object of Love" record similar resentment at God's seeming failure to live up to His end of the bargain. The intent in all three cases is not only to defy God but to hurt the ego as well. The ultimate motivation in such action is obscure. But Dostoyevski and Gide provide a clue. When humiliated, whether by God or another person, one bolsters one's pride and declares one's independence by hurting oneself. It is a way of asserting in action the words so often spoken by Freeman's characters: "I won't be beholden to anybody." Thus the poetess in the story deprives herself of her sole satisfaction, the writing of verse, and dies asserting her self-hood. On her deathbed she requests that the minister bury the ashes of her poems in her grave and compose a poem in her memory. When he asks why she destroyed her work, she tartly answers: "I found out it wa'n't worth nothin'" (158). But the minister fails to realize that the words are intended to make him feel guilty. He has no idea that he was the cause of her action, and the poetess is deprived of even that revenge. Yet she does achieve a minor triumph, that of becoming the subject of a poem by a poet supposedly her superior.[16] The poetess dies unreconciled, still bitter.

In "A Solitary" the recluse Nicholas Gunn achieves a reconciliation with God, against whom he has rebelled. Nicholas has lost his beloved wife, and he has suffered other unspecified sorrows and calamities, mainly from folks he "set by" (231). He devises a novel solution for getting the better of a cheating life:

I figured out that if I didn't care anything for anybody, I shouldn't have no trouble from 'em; an' if I didn't care anything for myself, I shouldn't have any from myself. . . . I let folks alone. . . , an' didn't do anything for myself. I kept cold when I wanted to be warm, an' warm when I wanted to be cold. I didn't eat anything I liked, an' I left things around that hurt me to see. My wife she made them wax flowers an' them gimcracks [in the room where he is talking]. Then I used to read the Bible, 'cause I used to believe in it an' didn't now, an' it made me feel worse. I did about everything I could to spite myself. . . . (231–32)

Nicholas pursues his masochistic way in an unheated cottage on a lonely mountainside. His diet is cornmeal mush and water. On blizzardy days he sits on his doorsteps while the snow piles up on him as if he were one of the boulders in his fields. When a neighbor, sick and exhausted, stops on his way up the mountain to ask for a moment of warmth and shelter, Nicholas surlily permits him to enter the fireless kitchen but does nothing for his comfort. The question is: What can bring Nicholas out of his self-loathing and reinstate him as a member of the human race from which he has seceded? Whereas in medieval Europe, Freeman points out, he might have been popularly venerated as a saintly hermit, he is here the object of a scorn that only deepens his misanthropy. The way out of his dilemma is perhaps sentimental but one that the sages of most religions, as well as the psychiatrists of our day, agree upon as almost the sole cure for a sickness like Nicholas's. Love is the sovereign remedy for such ills, and Nicholas benefits from it as much as any one else. Freeman's formula is precisely that of Dostoyevski. The self-laceration resulting from the humiliation of the ego terminates only when, through love, one transforms humiliation into humility.

So it is with Nicholas Gunn. Another day the neighbor stops to rest at the hut, but this time he is so ill that Nicholas permits him to remain longer and ministers to his comfort. For years Nicholas has used his stove only to cook his mush. Now he lights it to warm his house. With this symbolic act, spiritual thaw sets in. Nicholas invites the ailing old man to live with him. He redirects his energies from self-hurt to helping another. He even begins to feed the sparrows that hop about on the snow outside his house. As one critic has pointed out, he is transformed from a churl to a mother figure.[17]

The Healthy Will

In a number of stories in *A New England Nun,* as in *A Humble Romance,* a strong but healthy will is directed toward constructive ends that it eventually attains after severe struggle. These are manifestations of the Puritan will at its best; they are proof of its original vigor. "Louisa" is such a story, and it is one of the most skillfully written in the volume. It celebrates the independence of a young countrywoman—a teacher who has lost her job through the nepotism of a school committeeman. She refuses to marry a rich suitor, as her widowed mother desires, but devotes herself to wresting a living from the single acre of land the family owns. Among numerous handicaps that she has to overcome is her senile grandfather, who digs up her seed potatoes as fast as she plants them. When not cultivating her own land, she hires herself out as a fieldworker, much to the chagrin of her mother, who is shocked at the idea of a New England girl doing outdoor labor for pay.

Louisa is a finely drawn character, reminiscent of Dorinda Oakley in Ellen Glasgow's *Barren Ground.* Her independence seems as natural as the plants that grow out of the soil she tills; one can admire her refusal to marry her wealthy but arrogant suitor. The story ranks high among Freeman's stories that deal with pride among the rural poor, and in this case the pride is not pathological. Even the happy ending, in which the suitor marries the woman who had usurped Louisa's teaching job and thus makes available to Louisa this source of much-needed income, is acceptable.

"A Church Mouse" deals with the same theme in a lighter manner. Hetty Fifield, having been turned out of the house where she had been living and working for years, decides that she would like to have the job of sexton in the village church. She cajoles the deacon into letting her have the position; and, against his better judgment, she moves her stove and bed into the meetinghouse to live there. The congregation tolerate her for a while, for they could not turn her out as "they would a Jersey cow. They had their Puritan consciences . . ." (415). But their patience is exhausted when during meeting the mephitic odor of cooking cabbage drifts through the building. The selectmen wait upon the sexton as a group, but fail in their efforts to remove her. The minister goes to get his wife, for whose powers of persuasion he has learned to entertain a high regard. On returning, however, he finds that Hetty has barricaded herself into the church as into a blockhouse. The minister's wife, in a show of feminine solidarity, takes Hetty's side. Forced to negotiate with her, the selectmen end by permitting her to remain. On the next day, which is Christmas, Hetty rings the church bells in celebration of the Nativity, the first time they have ever been heard in this Puritan town.

Another story in *A New England Nun,* "Christmas Jenny," is also a Christmas story—a genre in which Freeman made many contributions to *Harper's Bazar.* But in addition to carrying a message appropriate to the season, this story portrays one of the most likable and interesting of Freeman's eccentric independent-minded women and also makes some penetrating comments on New England village attitudes. Christmas Jenny (or Jenny Wrayne, her somewhat sentimentally conceived real name) lives on a mountainside high above a village, whose inhabitants consider her to be "love-cracked," that is, rendered queer by disappointment in love. But in fact she has found a substitute for love or marriage. Earning her living by selling Christmas greens from her woods and vegetables from her garden, she has dedicated herself to the feeding of wild animals and birds and caring for them when injured. Her cabin is full of caged creatures of many species, and with her lives a little deaf and mute child whom she has rescued from the hell of a poor farm. But she also befriends a neighboring woman, successfully aiding her in dealing with a particularly difficult, stubborn husband. Though this thread in the story provides a measure of comedy, it is a striking example of the way women support each other in much of Freeman's fiction.

All this reveals Jenny as an admirable person, but—and here Freeman makes a very negative point about New England communities—
the villagers darkly hint that this female St. Francis is torturing her
caged animals and birds and is mistreating the young boy. Puzzled by
a selflessness and charity that their professed religion teaches, they believe "the town" (in the centuries-old connotation of the term as em-
bodying a singleness of purpose and opinion) should intervene. In this
case the church, representing "the town," does the intervening. Jenny's
fault is that she has deviated from the normally expected behavior of a
"love-cracked" woman. Instead of settling down to a lifetime as a seamstress in a cottage on the village street, she has gone into the woods
and done all sorts of unspinsterish things. Thus the local minister, a
mild old man, and his deacon, who is young and not mild, trudge up
the mountain, find Jenny is not at home, enter her cabin, and inspect
the interior. Whether Marjorie Pryse is correct in saying this is an
intrusion on Jenny's sexuality,[18] it surely is an intrusion on her privacy
and her human dignity. Freeman interprets it in terms of Puritanism,
as she does with the characters and action in many of her early stories,
much to the deepening of their meaning. Of the minister and the
deacon, she writes:

Indeed, everything out of the broad, common track was a horror to these men
and to many of their village fellows. Strange shadows, that their eyes could
not pierce, lay upon such, and they were suspicious. The popular sentiment
against Jenny Wrayne was originally the outcome of this characteristic, which
was a remnant of the old New England witchcraft superstition. More than
anything else, Jenny's eccentricity, her possibly uncanny deviation from the
ordinary ways of life, had brought this inquiry upon her. In actual meaning,
although not even in self-acknowledgment, it was a witchhunt that went up
the mountain road that December afternoon. (173–74)

This is not the only or the last instance in which Freeman reveals an
interest in witchcraft and an understanding of it.

Of course, since it is a Christmas story, "Christmas Jenny" ends
happily. The intruders into Jenny's hut receive a deserved tongue-lash-
ing from the neighbor woman whom Jenny had befriended. Totally
contrite and abashed—male dominance is routed here—they retire
down the mountain; and the townspeople, in a reversal of feeling, lav-
ish Jenny with gifts. But within the confines of a potentially mawkish
genre, Freeman has made one of her most profound statements about

the rural society in which she spent the great part of her life and about which she did her best writing.

"Amanda and Love"

In a category by itself in *A New England Nun* is the story "Amanda and Love," in which Freeman probes with deep psychological insight the relationship of two sisters. Amanda, the elder, is a stiff, curt, hardworking spinster who keeps her sister, Love, an adult but young enough to be her daughter, under a relentless surveillance. They live in a tiny cottage with a couple of acres of land on a village street—a standard dwelling for Freeman's widows and spinsters; and they eke out a living by sewing and by selling vegetables grown on their little plot of land. Money not needed for bare subsistence goes for clothes and minor luxuries for Love, who occupies the larger of the two bedchambers. Amanda's affection for her sister is of the smothering kind that deprives its object of any freedom of action or thought. It is, in fact, a selfish love; for Amanda, who is gaunt and plain, sees in her sister, who is less plain and quite well-dressed, a mirror image of herself—or herself as she might have wished to be. Essentially, the elder sister has devoured the younger's life.

Amanda has apparently never had any thoughts of marriage, nor has she ever had any suitors, but Love has caught the attention of a young man, and he has been calling on her. Amanda, of course, is jealous, but her main emotion is fear—fear, actually, of losing the part of herself that the girl has become. On one of the young man's visits, Amanda meets him at the door and, as Freeman admirably puts it, asks him "to lay aside his hat and coat in very much the same way that she might have asked an enemy to lay down his arms" (295). During the visit Amanda monopolizes the conversation, and as a result the youth leaves disgruntled and does not reappear thereafter on his accustomed Wednesday evenings. Love, incredibly weak as she is, remains docile, but goes into a decline that seems to threaten consumption. After sleepless nights of fierce inner struggle, in which she wrestles "with a problem of nature" (299)—her sister's sexuality—Amanda undergoes one of those conversionlike changes of heart so common with Freeman's characters. Humbling herself, she begs Love's suitor to renew his visits; he does so, and all goes smoothly with him and Love. Amanda has accomplished the feat of replacing her selfishness with selflessness.

On her way back from begging Love's swain to return, Amanda hears frogs croaking in a pond, and Freeman remarks, "They would have seemed to her like the chorus in a Greek tragedy had she ever heard of one" (303). It has been suggested that this story is a "Yankee tragedy," and in a way it is.[19] Freeman comments: "People when they overstep their bounds of conduct are apt to step high and wide; poor Amanda had cleared hers well" (303) and, as in classic tragedy, she is chastened for her excess. But by another interpretation the story may be taken as an allegory. Freeman makes it clear that Amanda has identified herself with her sister; but her sister is named Love and has fallen into the clutches of sexual love, which Freeman calls "a problem of nature." Amanda (whose name, incidentally, means "must be loved") has suppressed her own sexuality just as she has regulated every aspect of her sister's life. Of course, suppression of a natural force like that of sex may have tragic results, as the hero of Euripides' play *Hyppolytus* learned at the cost of his life. Amanda's efforts to ignore her own or Love's sexuality end in a near disaster—the death of Love—averted only by Amanda's recognition that she was dealing with a force too powerful for even a strong-willed New England spinster to control. Nature cannot be thwarted.

Assessment

In *A Humble Romance* and *A New England Nun* Freeman presents a comprehensive and consistent appraisal of New England village life. Contrary to what certain critics and literary historians have said, she does not unconditionally condemn this way of life as narrow and soul-killing. Though critical, she does not belong in that literary movement labeled "The Revolt from the Village," which includes such authors as Hamlin Garland and Sinclair Lewis. Nor does she wage mortal warfare on vestigial Puritanism. She sees the shortcomings of rural New England character, but she is also aware of its strengths, which also have their roots in Puritanism. As a general thing the people in her fiction are free to work out their destinies by their own devices. Sometimes they become warped, but that is not so damning to the social order as an adherence to a standardized pattern of character would be. Some stories, of course, reveal the evils of gossip and the villagers' intolerance and misunderstanding of any major deviation from the norm.

In summary, the following seem to be the major points in Freeman's evaluation of New England village life:

1. It is often afflicted with poverty, which arouses great distress in Freeman and some indignation against the industrialization and other forces that have brought it about. Her country people seldom sit down to a full-course meal except at Thanksgiving. Usually their fare consists of a bowl of soup or a cup of tea and bread or a serving of cornmeal mush. The poorhouse is a repeatedly presented evidence of this poverty.

2. Life is often monotonous and lonely, and spinsterhood and celibacy are common conditions.

3. In these circumstances people may, but not always, become ingrown, and some may become bigoted, backbiting, or surly.

4. Some characters assert their independence of the rest of the community and, even though they are branded as "peculiar," succeed in living meaningfully.

5. The townspeople themselves often recognize the intrinsic value of this type of struggle and respect it even when it results in oddness.

6. To offset the loneliness of the lives of so many of the villagers there is among them a solidarity, based on their commonly shared beliefs and widespread participation in church and town government, that gives even the most inveterate solitary the security that arises from a consciousness of "belonging." In such closely knit societies, something usually can be arranged to alleviate the distress of all but the most abysmally unfortunate.

7. Because women outnumber men, the rural towns have become quasi-matriarchies, though tradition and popular mores exclude women from many activities, including church and local governance. Yet in mind and will the women are stronger than the men, and they frequently break out of their socially sanctioned roles. The conflict of wills thus generated provides the psychological tensions that make Freeman's fiction interesting.

Given these conditions, both favorable and unfavorable, the central theme of Freeman's village fiction is the struggle of the individual toward self-fulfillment, whether in marriage, on the farm, in the pulpit, or in the schoolhouse. The environment is a hard one in which to achieve self-realization, and many persons fail; but others are tougher than the environment, and their success speaks well for Yankee tenacity. As Susan Toth has written, "Many of [Freeman's] characters suffer, but they also fight their way to significant victories. Living in drab poverty, they still struggle with courageous spirit towards self-expression and independence."[20]

The critical reception of *A New England Nun* was generally favorable.

Typical were the remarks in an article in the *Atlantic Monthly* of June 1891 in which the anonymous reviewer discusses Freeman's book along with collections of stories by Annie Trumbull Slosson and Sarah Orne Jewett. Among these three, the reviewer finds Freeman to be the most successful in conveying a feeling for the loneliness of New England rural life and in delineating the remarkably individualized characters—"highly intensified and noticeable persons, though the exaggerations may be of unimportant qualities"[21]—fostered by the religious and political conditions of the region. The writer praises Freeman's fiction for its lack of sentimentality, its extreme compression, and its reproduction, without resort to phonetic transcription, of the speech of New England countryfolk.

Chapter Four
The Will

Since the 1880s Freeman has been praised as an anatomist of the latter-day Puritan will. The question of human volition, its freedom from or its dependence on divine decree, had for centuries been a preoccupation of Calvinists both in Europe and in America. Freeman, nurtured in traditional Congregationalism, which descended directly from the rigid Calvinism of the Reformation, inevitably approached the problem in terms of the theology that was at the very marrow of her training. To understand her approach, one must examine the religious doctrine in rural New England during her lifetime, especially her earlier years.

"Strenuous Goadings of Conscience"

In Freeman's day, Calvinistic orthodoxy had softened considerably. Throughout New England the old religion was in conflict with Unitarianism, which had gained control of many of the Congregational churches, especially in the cities. But a Calvinism only slightly modified was far from extinct in most of the villages, and nowhere in New England was its spirit dead. The New England conscience was no less a goad in directing the average life in accordance with the virtues always valued by the Puritans—duty, truthfulness, honesty, thrift. The Nicene Creed held unchallenged sway among those churches that had not gone over to Unitarianism. God was still in his heaven, ready to pass judgment on the deeds and thoughts of men and women, smiling or frowning upon their affairs as merited. Heaven awaited the righteous, hell the sinner. God's only son, Christ, was the sole means of salvation. Full membership as a communicant in a church was still deemed a requisite for eligibility in sharing the benefits of Christ's atonement. Admission to church membership, in turn, depended on the applicant's proof before a board of elders that he or she had undergone the experience of conversion, that is, an overwhelming, emotionally charged surge of conviction of the reality of Christ and a consuming love of him.

Conversion was, and perhaps still is, the most important episode in
the life of any Christian in the sects deriving from Calvinism. Without
this all-engrossing sense of assurance that Christ lives in heaven and
earth and constitutes the sole access to the future life of the pious, any
spiritual advance was thought to be impossible. At all costs one must
undergo conversion. To aid the spiritually slothful to this end, periods
of revival were set aside each year in many New England villages in
the last century. Mary Ellen Chase in her autobiographical *A Goodly
Heritage* (1932) describes the annual revivals in Blue Hill, Maine, the
little coastal town in which she grew up. For weeks each winter, while
the drive for regeneration progressed, the young people of the town
would subject themselves to agonizing soul-searching. After several
alterations between ecstasy and despair, a person would usually announce the achievement of a state of grace—social and family pressures
would hardly allow another outcome—and the convert would be admitted to the Lord's Supper and, if male, to full participation in church
governance. From then on the convert would enjoy a well-founded
hope for life eternal. Persons remaining unaffected, despite the exhor-
tations of preachers, parents and friends who had made the grade, sank
into a state of self-accusing despair, which might later give way to
defiance.

    In the colleges, too, the students were annually lashed into similar
mass convulsions of the spirit. In Emily Dickinson's letters, for example, are accounts of revivals at Mount Holyoke Female Seminary
and of her own consequent agonizings over her inability to yield to
them. Never a convert in the orthodox sense, she may well have owed
much of the mental pain of her later life to this youthful worry over
her inner state. A careful reading of her letters reveals that Dickinson
never totally rejected the religion of her forefathers. In moments of
personal crisis she sought the advice and help of clergymen. Many of
her attitudes toward God were strictly Puritan, such as her demands
on Him that He live up to certain legalistic standards in His dealings
with the human species. Freeman also attended Mount Holyoke Seminary for one year; and in her era the revivals were still being held.
One reason that caused her to leave, "a nervous wreck," was "too strenuous goadings of the conscience,"[1] though she was already converted.

    New England Puritanism was always in some respects a peculiarly
public religion. Those who had seriously erred were often required to
make public confession before regaining full standing in the church.
Revivals, of course, were and are entirely public; and the state of one's

soul becomes readily evident by whether or not one proclaims oneself converted. Each person's sins and degree of grace were the concern of the entire community in New England of a hundred or so years ago. Small wonder that the villages seethed with gossip and that the church itself sanctioned and encouraged speculation as to the inner and outer life of each of its members or would-be members. No wonder that fears of what one's neighbors might think were pivotal in determining one's decisions. Always, it must be emphasized, one's conduct was an indication of the state of one's soul.

According to the strictest Calvinism one was among either the elect, that is, those destined for salvation, or those slated for eternal damnation. From the beginning of time one's name was in God's book for one of these destinies. One's personal efforts were to no avail; the doctrine of good works was deemed a heresy. But the elect, with the help of the church, could expect to experience conversion and after conversion lead sanctified lives—moral, useful, frugal, righteous ones. They could also expect to prosper in their calling, enjoying more material wealth than their unsanctified fellows. On the other hand, failure to experience conversion and lead a prosperous and righteous life indicated that one had been abandoned by God and was bound for everlasting punishment as the just result of Adam's sin perpetuated through all generations.

How desirable it was, therefore, that one's life appear Godly and prosperous! No one wished to pass as one of the abandoned of God. Even the converted had to watch their actions, for the genuineness of any conversion was never totally certain. Any moral backsliding or loss of money or standing could be construed as an indication that one's conversion had been spurious. In the Puritan community there was no resting on the certainty of conversion. Constant soul-searching, as exemplified in the writing of such eminent Puritans as Cotton Mather and Jonathan Edwards, was the norm for the inner life. Did one's business or farm flourish? Did one become an elder in the church or a selectman in the town government? Did one's family multiply and remain healthy? If the answers to such questions were positive, then one had the satisfaction of assuming all was well as far as God was concerned and of knowing that one's fellow townspeople had the same assumption. But if one's house burned, or one's cattle proved barren, or the voters ejected one from office, then one would be gripped with mortal apprehension and neighbors would speculate somberly regarding one's chances of salvation.

This state of affairs may be exaggerated in this brief description, but it is reasonably true even for so late a period as the second half of the nineteenth century. To a certain extent it is true also for today, if one places credence in the theories of such writers as R. H. Tawney and Max Weber concerning the "Protestant ethic." At all events, the Calvinist outlook placed a premium upon success. It encouraged strenuous effort and exertion in reaching a goal that would impress one's neighbors and convince oneself of God's favor.

A curious paradox, however, exists in Calvinism, and therefore a huge section of Protestantism, regarding the will. Taken at face value, the doctrines of election and predestination would seem to nullify the will. If one were not chosen, all the willpower in the world would be to no avail. But theologians, seeking a way out of this dilemma, asserted that, even though God knows what a person's volition will be, that person still has freedom of will. According to this theory, the human will is still a significant agent. As Jonathan Edwards stated in the eighteenth century, volitions "are necessary events,"[2] necessary because God knows they will occur; but since they are part of God's plan for the universe, these volitions must be vigorously exerted.[3]

Emerson: "In the will work and acquire"

The great paradox of New England Protestantism, then, was that while its basic Calvinism was deterministic, strongly minimizing one's ability to shape one's own destiny by one's own will, yet it actually made the will the most important human faculty. The average New Englander, moreover, was thoroughly conversant in the various theories of the will. Oliver Wendell Holmes has pointed out that a churchgoing New Englander received during his lifetime the equivalent of a college education in doctrine by reading theological tracts and by listening to innumerable sermons,[4] one of the favorite topics of which was the will and its freedom or lack of freedom. Trained in a first-rate divinity school like those in Bangor and Andover, any village minister would have been only too eager to pass on his learning to his congregation.

In the nineteenth century, transcendentalist thinking about the will had the result of enhancing the prominence already accorded it by the orthodox. Emerson's works were being read widely, especially such essays as "Self-Reliance" and "Compensation," and Emerson was one of Freeman's "spiritual fathers."[5] The concluding passage of "Self-Reliance" exalts the human will to the level of the Godhead: "Most men gamble with [fortune] and gain all, and lose all, as her wheel rolls. But do thou leave as unlawful these winnings, and deal with Cause and Effect, the chancellors of God. In the Will work and acquire, and thou hast chained the wheel of Chance. . . ."[6] This concept seems to be nondeterministic.

On the other hand, in his essay on "Fate" in *The Conduct of Life* Emerson leans toward a benign determinism. Human beings share in the eternal mind (the oversoul), Emerson argues; thus their minds, being a particle of God's, control the material forces of cause and effect. The individual's share in the oversoul must be in harmony with the whole, which is obviously self-governing. Thus the individual will, when untrammeled, is carrying out the divine will, in which it shares, and one is free to do the oversoul's will. God's will and the individual's are the same, and both are good. Emerson's conclusion is thus essentially the same as Saint Augustine's: true freedom lies in the inability to do evil. Emerson writes:

He who sees through the design, presides over it, and must will that which must be. We sit and rule, and, though we sleep, our dream will come to pass. Our thought, though it were only an hour old, affirms an oldest necessity, not to be separated from thought, and not to be separated from will. They must always have coexisted. . . . It is not mine or thine, but the will of all mind. It is poured into the souls of all men, as the soul itself which constitutes them men. . . . A breath of will blows eternally through the universe of souls in the direction of the Right and Necessary.[7]

Emerson's remarks are reminiscent of Jonathan Edward's views. One "must will that which must be" sounds almost Calvinistic. So does the following from the same essay: "The tendency of every man to enact all that is in his constitution is expressed in the old belief that the efforts which we make to escape from our destiny only serve to lead us into it."[8] Paraphrased in Calvinist terms these statements mean simply that the converted, come what may, will inevitably persevere to the salvation for which they have been elected, and those who have not been elected will just as inevitably work for their own damnation. Any efforts these unfortunates make to escape their damnation will serve only to lead them into it—even if their efforts are backed by the last jot of the will's energy. Finally, Emerson's statement that "a man's fortunes are the fruit of his character"[9] echoes the Calvinist assumption that the elect will be righteous and prosper and the abandoned will be wicked and grow poor. "I have noticed," he continues, "that a man likes better to be complimented on his position, as the proof of the last or total excellence, than on his merits."[10] Thus Emerson, entangled in the perennial New England controversy over the freedom of the will, argued himself back into a position not fundamentally different from that of the strictest orthodoxy.

An "Awful Will"

From the earliest times and through the nineteenth century in New England, the will had been not only a subject of discussion but an object of cultivation. For the settlement of a wilderness, a vigorous will combined with a sense of mission (that is, a conviction that the divine will and the human will coincide in their purposes) was invaluable. The first settlements were obviously established by sheer perseverance. And the later waves of immigration that settled the hill farms and founded hundreds of back-country villages were energized by the same irresistible willpower. Among American writers Freeman is the supreme analyst of the Puritan will in its constructive strengths, in its aberrations, and in its decadence into mere whim and stubbornness. The will is the subject of scores of her stories and of all her major novels. The theme of these works is the general one that the will among the Puritans and their descendants is prone to overdevelopment and can be rechanneled into useful courses only by a struggle resulting in emotional change so sudden and violent as to resemble religious conversion. The stories already discussed provide many examples of Freeman's treatment of the will, but it is worthwhile to examine one single story solely as an illustration of her ideas on the subject. Of a hundred possible choices, "A Conflict Ended" from *A Humble Romance* is typical.

In the simple plot, Marcus Woodman has strongly objected to the appointment by the local Congregational church of a minister who is not "doctrinal" (389). Rashly, he vows that he will spend his Sabbaths sitting on the meetinghouse steps rather than attend worship conducted by such a parson. Someone retorts that he will have to sit there fifty years then. Indeed, as the story opens, he has been sitting there summer and winter during Sunday meetings for ten years, a victim of his "awful will" (397). His fiancée, the dressmaker Esther Barney, also has a formidable will. Refusing to marry someone who is making a fool of himself—she is very sensitive to village opinion—she breaks the engagement. A strange relationship develops between the two. Far from becoming enemies, they inwardly remain very fond of each other, despite their outer antagonism. As she enters the church each Sunday morning, Esther inquires after Marcus's mother; and, if it is sunny, she offers him the use of her parasol, which he refuses. Yet they can never be married unless a complete reversal occurs in the course each one is pursuing.

Esther changes first. Her young apprentice, Margy, has had a falling out with her own lover and for a time proudly refuses a reconciliation. But finally Margy humbles her pride and takes the necessary first step that restores her life to happiness. Thus it is suggested to Esther that she might take the initiative in approaching Marcus. Many objections stand in the way of her decision. She is resentful of the ridicule that Marcus has brought upon himself. She is not sure that he still cares for her sufficiently to marry her. She has become so "set" in her spinster's ways that she hesitates to change them by marriage. After much inner conflict she gives in and tells Marcus that she will wed him even if he continues his "sit-in" on the church porch.

The will that carried Esther through ten years of stubborn opposition was so strong that only by furious struggle could she overcome it. But once the reversal is achieved, she persists in her new course with equal inflexibility. Thus they are married. The Sunday after the wedding the two climb the church steps and Marcus hesitates:

> "Oh, Esther, I've—got—to stop."
> "Well, we'll both sit down here, then."
> "*You?*"
> "Yes; I'm willing."
> "No; you go in."
> "No, Marcus; I sit with you on our wedding Sunday."

Her sharp middle-aged face as she looked up at him was fairly heroic. This was all that she could do: her last weapon was used. If this failed, she would accept the chances with which she had married, and before the eyes of all these tittering people she would sit down at his side on these church steps. She was determined, and she would not weaken. (397–98)

Marcus's struggle had been more dire than Esther's had been; in tears he had confessed to her, when she offered to marry him, that his life had been a misery, that he now knew he would have given all he had to have got up any one of the Sundays in the past and walked into the church. But he had been unable to; he "ain't made strong enough to"

(396). So the Sunday when the newlyweds hesitate on the church steps is critical in Marcus's life. But the reversal—the conversion, so to speak—occurs: "He stood for a moment staring into her face. He trembled so that the bystanders noticed it. He actually leaned over towards his old seat as if wire ropes were pulling him down upon it. Then he stood up straight, like a man, and walked through the church door with his wife. The people followed. Not one of them even smiled. They had felt the pathos in the comedy" (398). The change in Marcus has been complete and instantaneous. It was in this way that Freeman conceived that the New England will operated. Its actions had, for her, the same decisiveness and finality in daily as in religious life. By struggling for the right, the will could achieve it, just as within the Puritan paradox. Though limited by God, the human will was God's chief tool in achieving his end, which in turn should be man's or woman's end.[11]

Freeman was not the first nor the only author to analyze the functioning, both beneficent and harmful, of the Puritan will. Actually she was writing within a well-established New England literary tradition, represented by Sarah Orne Jewett and Nathaniel Hawthorne, both of whom explored manifestations of the will or conscience in their fictional characters. Thus Hawthorne in *The Scarlet Letter* had drawn the frightening portrait of Roger Chillingworth, a man whose life is governed by the single grim volition of discovering, and taking his revenge upon, his wife's seducer. Chillingworth himself, in moments of insight, becomes appalled at the hold his unholy purpose has upon him and wonders if he is not acting out some predestined role and whether or not his will is the instrument of a greater power than he is. Just as Marcus Woodman feels himself constrained by wires, so Chillingworth feels himself in a bondage outside his control. "My old faith, long forgotten," he says, "comes back to me. . . . It has all been a dark necessity."[12] Likewise Hollingsworth in Hawthorne's *The Blithedale Romance* becomes so much a slave to his life's purpose of reforming criminals that he excludes from his character such human indispensables as tolerance, sympathy, and love. Indeed, the dehumanization of the heart that afflicts so many of Hawthorne's characters is the result of a wrongly directed but virtually irresistible will; such is Dr. Rappaccini's fanatical devotion to science or Ethan Brand's fanatical search for the unpardonable sin.

Writers of lesser magnitude than Hawthorne but closer to Freeman in subject matter, technique, and settings were Harriet Beecher Stowe

(1811–96) and Rose Terry Cooke (1827–92), both of whom wrote about New England rural folk, some of them possessors of wills as stubborn and "cussed" as that of Marcus Woodman. Examples are Zeph Higgins, a Connecticut farmer, in Stowe's *Poganuc People* (1878) and Cooke's Freedom Wheeler in the story "Freedom Wheeler's Controversy with Providence" (1877).

Chapter Five

Three Novels on the Will and the Conscience

Jane Field

In January 1893 Freeman published her first novel in book form, the tragicomedy *Jane Field*. It had previously been serialized in *Harper's New Monthly,* and with the final installment in November 1892 appeared a full-page portrait of Freeman, still looking young and almost pert despite her forty years. "The Editor's Easy Chair" of the same issue contained words of praise for the novel and its author's natural diction, spontaneity, and realism. Freeman's art, the editor opined, was not the result of formal education. No one told her how to write. Not a mere recorder of observations, she transfers to her pages images generated by her fancy and her inward perceptions, much as the old balladists produced their verses. "Nothing in the history of literature stands so entirely by itself as the career of this demure New England maiden."[1]

The action of *Jane Field* begins in the back-country town of Green River, a half day by rail from Boston and obviously modeled on one of the towns near Brattleboro. The setting of the latter part of the novel is in Elliot, just outside Boston and highly suggestive of Randolph. The widow Jane Field lives with her ailing daughter Lois, whose job as teacher in the village school constitutes their sole means of support, though at such a place at that time her salary could have been no more than five dollars a week. Convinced by busybody neighbors that Lois is suffering from consumption, Jane Field is in despair. A letter from a lawyer in Elliot addressed to her recently dead sister announces that the sister's father-in-law has left her his very substantial estate. In case the sister is not living, the inheritance goes to the daughter of another of the old man's sons.

Jane Field, a woman of granite will and purpose, decides to impersonate her sister, whom she closely resembles, and claims the legacy; for there is no other way of getting the funds needed to restore her daughter's health. She is an offspring of the Puritans, a devout church-goer, possessed of a sensitive conscience as well as of a powerful voli-tion. Thus an elaborate rationalization precedes the imposture she is planning. She justifies her course by the fact that she had loaned her sister's husband $1,500 that he had never paid back. She would take that sum of money and not a cent more. She concludes: "Everybody ought to have what's their just due. . . . Folks ought to lay hold of justice themselves if there ain't no other way, an' that's what we've got hands for."[2]

Thus determined, Jane Field sets off for Elliot, where she deceives the lawyer and the whole town, including many relatives of her sister's husband, into believing that she is the rightful heir. But on her first night in Elliot, alone in the big house that is part of the inheritance, she suffers pangs of conscience. She does not go to bed but sits up in the darkness. "Gradually this steady-minded, unimaginative old woman became possessed by a legion of morbid fancies, which played like wild fire over the terrible main fact of the case—the fact that underlay everything—that she had sinned, that she had gone over from good to evil, and given up her soul for a handful of gold" (92). For the next few months, during which she is joined by her daughter, her existence is a life-and-death struggle between her will and her sense of having made a choice for evil. To assuage her conscience, she is careful to eat none of the food that is in the house but subsists largely on berries and on eggs from chickens she has purchased. Also, she gives away many household articles to the mother of the rightful heiress. Thus her reason tells her she is doing right; she will take only the equivalent of what is justly hers and then somehow hand over the rest to the legal owner. To carry on in this painful position she exerts her powerful will: "I'm a-followin' out my own law an' my own right," she tells her daughter. "I ain't ashamed of it. If you want to be you can" (169). As Freeman puts it, "Although fairly started forth in the slough of deceit, she still held up her Puritan skirts arduously" (137).

According to orthodox New England thought from the seventeenth century to the end of the nineteenth, the will working alone in the presence of its creator was considered the prime mover of lives. One must use the will to do right, to avoid sin. Nothing worthwhile is accomplished except by mighty travail of the will. The harder one tries to do right, as conscience directs, the more godly one is. Effort itself is a sign of grace. That one is frequently confronted with conflicting objects of the will is not surprising; the Devil entices in one direction and God in another, and it is not always easy to tell which is which. But the choice must finally be made. Jane Field's dilemma is the classical Puritan one.

Outbursts of emotion normally accompany any act of will that sweeps one into a wholly new path, say, that of conversion. Most Puritan divines, such as Jonathan Edwards, recognized this. It is as if the will needs a sudden last surcharge of energy to make its irreversible plunge forward. Jane Field has shown herself prone to such outbursts. The violent act of volition that sent her off to Elliot bent on subterfuge was preceded by an almost barbaric fit of grief for her daughter, who had been carried home after fainting on the village street. The residue of this passion encased her as in armor while she went about executing her plan: "Her own nature had grown so intense that it apparently had emanations, and surrounded her with an atmosphere of her own impenetrable to the world" (69). The volcanic, passionate core of the outwardly restrained New England character is well illustrated in this woman.

But imposture is of course a sin; and though initially espoused by the will and sanctioned by the reason, it must ultimately be abandoned by all but the most irretrievably lost. Jane Field is not among the unredeemable. One summer afternoon while she is berrying, a violent thunderstorm overtakes her. The storm is an accurate reflection of the turmoil within her own soul. Arriving home, she finds three friends from Green River have come to see her; not knowing the desperate part she is playing, they constitute an inadvertent jeopardy to her hitherto successful impersonation. Even though a week passes without divulgence of her secret—all this is incredible to the reader—Jane Field is approaching the turning point. Having chosen the path of sin, she now reverses herself, and with equally merciless lashings of her will she drives herself to repentance.

"Jane Field lay awake all night. Suddenly at dawn she formed a plan; her mind was settled. There was seemingly no struggle. It was to her as if she had turned a corner, once turned there was no other way, and no question about it" (248). But if her decision is taken in calmness, the volcano erupts that afternoon. Her voice rises "to a stern shriek" (259) as she informs her friends that she "ain't Esther Maxwell," her sister. Not content to confess only to her cronies, she parades up and down the street stopping the townspeople and knocking at doors to tell the world she "ain't Mrs. Maxwell." Here is the equivalent of conversion—the paroxysm, the remorse, the life that suddenly reverses its direction, all revealed to the eyes of the gaping public. Having seen her error in taking it on herself "to do justice instead of the Lord" (259), Jane Field can do no less than spend the summer informing the countryside of her sin. To the New Englander for several centuries one's sins and one's repentance for them were matters of public concern. The eyes of the townspeople were as searching and as critical as those of God.

But with Jane Field, as with many of Freeman's characters, "the stern will of the New England woman had warped her whole nature into one groove" (266). She now *overpays* for her sin. Her state is one of psychopathy rather than of grace. All the rest of her life she continues to announce that she "ain't Mrs. Maxwell." As Foster suggests, she may well have been modeled after one of the inmates of the state asylum near which the Wilkins family lived in Brattleboro.[3]

As a story *Jane Field* is a failure. The author too boldly violates the canons of credibility. But it is a success as a presentation of New England village life and character. Green River is the residual type of community found in the New England hills—a mere remnant of the teeming, hopeful settlement it once was. It has its school, its church, its town functionaries. There is even a railroad only a mile away. But if the census figures for all such towns hold true for Green River, it has now (in the novel) no more than half its population of sixty years earlier. And since the farms up in the hills have been for the most part abandoned, it is no longer a market center; and Jane Field's grinding poverty, as well as that of her friends, is typical. Neighbor is driven to meanness against neighbor in trying to secure whatever jobs are available. Thus a school board member uses Lois's illness as a pretext to replace her as teacher by his own daughter, so necessary to him is her wretched wage. The three townswomen are able to visit Jane Field in Elliot only because the railroad is offering a week's excursion to Boston for $3.60. So fundless are they that they forgo their lunches between trains. The outing was indeed the great event in the lives of these mature women. One of them had never been to Boston before. Another, a housewife descended from a line of ministers, is able to absent herself only after a painful searching of her conscience; her pleasure strikes her as materially and spiritually unfeasible: "'Well, I dunno but I've been pretty faithful, an' minded my household the way women are enjoined to in the Scriptures; mebbe it's right for me to take this little vacation,' she said, and her serious eyes were full of tears" (217). Of course, this woman's qualms are traceable not only to her religion but to the generally accepted notions, unquestioned by her, that her village society had about housewives' duties.

Pembroke: Village Gossip

Do you see that house? . . . the one with the front windows boarded up, without any step to the front door? Well, Barney Thayer lives there all alone. He's old Caleb Thayer's son, all the son that's left; the other one died. There was some talk of his mother's whippin' him to death. She died right after, but they said afterwards that she didn't, that he run away one night, an' went slidin' downhill, an' that was what killed him; he'd always had heart trouble. I dunno; I always thought Deborah Thayer was a pretty good woman, but she was pretty set. I guess Barney takes after her. He was goin' with Charlotte Barnard years ago—I guess 'twas as much as nine or ten years ago, now—an' they were goin' to be married. She was all ready—weddin'-dress an' bonnet an' everything'—an' this house was 'most done an' ready for them to move into; but one Sunday night Barney he went up to see Charlotte, an' he got into a dispute with her father about the 'lection, an' the old man he ordered Barney out of the house, an' Barney he went out, an' he never went in again— couldn't nobody make him. His mother she talked; it 'most killed her; an' I guess Charlotte said all she could, but he wouldn't stir a peg.

He went right to livin' in his new house, an' he lives there now; he ain't married, an' Charlotte ain't. She's had chances, too. Squire Payne's son, he wanted her bad.[4]

Such is the plot of *Pembroke* (1894), excepting its denouement, as told near the end of the novel by a village gossip to a friend from a neighboring town. Freeman had first heard the story as a child, for *Pembroke* is based on an incident in her mother's family, one that was still told after thirty years. Even the names of several of the persons in the real situation were transferred, with some reshuffling, to characters in the book. The house in which the Wilkinses lived in Randolph had been built by Freeman's grandfather, Barnabas Lothrop, for his son, Barnabas, Jr., who was to marry the local beauty, Mary Thayer. But the suitor and Mary's father got into a wrangle over politics, the younger man was ordered from the house never to return, and the match was broken off at the father's command. Neither man would yield, and Mary submitted to her father's will. Later Barnabas left town, and the unpainted house, nearer completion than in the novel, remained uninhabited for ten years. The old Barnabas gave it to his daughter Eleanor and her husband, Warren Wilkins. Freeman must have heard the story innumerable times and in much the same language as that of the gossip in the novel.

When Eleanor Wilkins told the story to her daughter, she explained the obstinacy of the two men by saying it was simply their way. But Freeman apparently was dissatisfied by this diagnosis. Now, years later, she was living again in Randolph, and she searched more closely for the motivation behind the perversity to which the house was a monument. The course that her own life was taking may have sensitized her perception. Already over forty, she was still single, still living as a boarder in a friend's house. Hanson Tyler had been a sustaining hope, and she may have been waiting for him as many of her fictional women waited for their absent and procrastinating lovers. But in 1892 word came that Tyler had married in California. For some years Freeman had been making extended visits in and near New York City, especially at Metuchen, New Jersey, in the household of Henry M. Alden, the editor of *Harper's New Monthly,* to which she had contributed many stories. During one of her sojourns with the Aldens at about this time, she met the man she was to marry eight years later. This was the hard-drinking, gay-living, horse-loving Dr. Charles Freeman, who in some respects, including his appearance, resembled Hanson Tyler. He held a degree in medicine from Columbia University's College of Physicians and Surgeons and had practiced several years as a medical examiner for the Bureau of Pensions in Washington, D.C., where he was reported to have lived a somewhat dissolute life. Either because of his way of life or for political reasons, or both, he was relieved of his duties in 1899 and returned to Metuchen to work in his family's coal and lumber business. In this small community he played a prominent social role and, possessing a discriminating taste in literature, was well received by the local group of intellectuals, many of whom worked in New York City. A strong attachment developed between him and the still pretty, middle-aged author from Massachusetts, and soon friends began to speculate concerning an engagement.[5]

Pembroke: Purposes

In the "Introductory Sketch" to a so-called "Biographical Edition" of *Pembroke* published by Harper in 1899, Freeman gives her most extensive statement of her views not only on this novel but on her writing in general. Some of her remarks are as follows:

Pembroke was originally intended as a study of the human will in several New England characters, in different phases of disease and abnormal development, and to prove, especially in the most marked case, the truth of a theory that its cure depended entirely on the capacity of the individual for a love which could rise above all consideration of self, as Barnabas Thayer's love for Charlotte Barnard finally did. . . .

When I make use of the term abnormal, I do not mean unusual in any sense. I am far from any intention to speak disrespectfully or disloyally of those stanch old soldiers of the faith who landed upon our inhospitable shores and laid the foundation, as on a very rock of spirit, for the New England of to-day; but I am not sure, in spite of their godliness, and their noble adherence, in the face of obstacles, to the dictates of their consciences, that their wills were not developed past the reasonable limit of nature. What wonder is it that their descendants inherit this peculiarity, though they may develop it for much less worthy and more trivial causes than the exiling themselves for a question of faith, even the carrying-out of personal and petty aims and quarrels?

There lived in a New England village, at no very remote time, a man who objected to the painting of the kitchen floor, and who quarrelled furiously with his wife concerning the same. When she persisted in spite of his wishes to the contrary, and the floor was painted, he refused to cross it to his dying day, and always to his great inconvenience, but probably to his soul's satisfaction, walked around it.

A character like this, holding to a veriest trifle with such a deathless cramp of the will, might naturally be regarded as a notable exception to a general rule; but his brethren who sit on a church steps during services, who are dumb to those whom they should love, and will not enter familiar doors because of quarrels over matters of apparently no moment, are legion. *Pembroke* is intended to portray a typical New England village of some sixty years ago, as many of the characters flourished at that time, but villages of a similar description have existed in New England at a much later date, and they exist to-day in a very considerable degree. . . .

There is often to a mind from the outside world an almost repulsive narrowness and a pitiful sordidness which amounts to tragedy in the lives of such people as those portrayed in *Pembroke*, but quite generally the tragedy exists only in the comprehension of the observer and not at all in that of the observed. The pitied would meet pity with resentment; they would be full of wonder and wrath if told their lives were narrow, since they have never seen the limit of the breadth of their current of daily life. A singing-school is as much to them as a symphony concert and grand opera to their city brethren, and a sewing church sociable as an afternoon tea. Though the standard of taste of the simple villagers, and their complete satisfaction therewith, may reasonably be lamented, as also their restricted view of life, they are not to be pitied, generally speaking, for their unhappiness in consequence. It may be that the lack of unhappiness constitutes the real tragedy.[6]

Pembroke: A Gallery of Grotesques—Barnabas

In *Pembroke* Freeman presents a gallery of grotesques comparable to that in Sherwood Anderson's *Winesburg, Ohio* (1919), which not only in its preoccupation with village-spawned abnormalities but also in style resembles Freeman's work more closely than any critic has yet noted. Barnabas Thayer is the most spectacular and the most painstakingly explored of the *Pembroke* characters. To begin with, Cephas Barnard, the man against whom Barnabas is pitted, is by no means a formidable adversary. Cephas is certainly stubborn and "set" in his ways, and given to making horrendous threats—which he usually backs down from. A militant vegetarian, he browbeats his family into eating sorrel pies, but this is as far as his despotism goes. His wife is more than a match for him, as is his daughter. The villagers regard him as a harmless eccentric. His theories about subduing the animal passions by abstaining from meat and warding off rheumatism by drinking gallons of water are laughable, though they betray his fears of sexuality, mainly perhaps in his daughter. Had Barnabas apologized two days after the argument, Cephas would have received him again as a visitor to his house and as the betrothed of Charlotte. In fact, Cephas, soon regretting the pain he had caused Charlotte by quarreling with her lover, goes to Barnabas himself in an endeavor to bring him back but is rebuffed.

Nor is Barnabas swayed by "what people will think," that merciless censor of the actions of all but the stoutest-hearted villagers. Freeman is careful to inform the reader that he is so aloof that he knows little and cares less about what people think. The reason he does not apologize to Cephas and win back Charlotte, whom he still loves and who still loves him, is that it never occurred to him that he could do so. Freeman states this explicitly and goes on to give reasons for Barnabas's singular blindness (19). Just before his dismissal from the Barnards' house he had been on the pinnacle of a happiness so ecstatic that he could attribute it only to God's grace. Now in his abysmal unhappiness he sees the same providence at work: "His natural religious bent, inherited from generations of Puritans, and kept in its channel by his training from infancy, made it impossible for him to conceive of sympathy or antagonism in its fullest sense apart from God" (18). The crushing of his happiness seems "to him settled and inevitable" (19), in other words, predestined; and all he can do is to exert his will in harmony with what he conceives of as God's will.

Of all Freeman's books *Pembroke* has been most often compared to Hawthorne's. Barnabas, indeed, is the most Hawthornesque of her characters. In *The Scarlet Letter,* when Roger Chillingworth has been pursuing his revenge for years, he admits to Hester that he could not desist if he wished. His course seems inevitable; his helplessness in its grip renews his belief in the fatalism of the Calvinist faith; he is acting according to what God has ordained. Similarly, Barnabas considers himself helpless in the toils of his obsession, which (as with Chillingworth's hunched back) has caused his spine to bend unnaturally in correspondence with his crooked will. When an acquaintance asks Barnabas if he has hurt his back, he replies: "I've hurt my soul. . . . It happened that Sunday night years ago. I—can't get over it." The acquaintance says: "I should think you'd better get over it. . . ." "I—can't," Barnabas replies (297).

From the first, in fact, Charlotte realizes that Barnabas is helpless, that he has "a terrible will that won't always let him do what he wants to himself (68). Occasionally, Barnabas struggles to break his distorted resolution. When he learns that Squire Payne's son is courting Charlotte, he can hardly endure the thought of losing her, which he considers a certainty. In one of his revolts against his fate—a rebelliousness that Freeman finds latent in the straitjacketed New England soul—he flings himself on the ground in a convulsive grief, groaning and sobbing and tearing up handfuls of grass.

Barnabas has been helpless from the start. His life becomes an allegory of the dehumanized heart, as do the lives of the fanatics in the writings of Hawthorne and Melville. The day after Barnabas breaks his engagement, he moves into his unfinished house—which now serves as a symbol of his own incomplete personality—and boards up most of the windows, thus shutting himself off physically and spiritually from human society. The curvature gradually becomes more noticeable in his spine until one winter he is bent double by a fierce attack of rheumatism brought on by frenzied woodchopping in a swamp. Through weeks of cold and snow and bitter winds that kept other men huddled at their hearths, he battled with the forest, itself symbolic of the Puritan heritage: "He stood from morning until night hewing down the trees, which had gotten their lusty growth from the graves of their own kind. Their roots were sunken deep among and twined about the very bones of their fathers which helped make up the rich frozen soil of the great swamp" (312).

Finally, as the villagers predicted, Barnabas becomes ill with rheumatic fever—the culmination of his spiritual sickness as well as of his physical exhaustion. Charlotte insists on nursing him despite the remonstrances of her family, who fear that her reputation will be compromised by her living alone in the house with the sick man. Though Barnabas realizes that he does not deserve these attentions, he is still too aloof from humankind to understand that Charlotte is laying herself open to the most vicious sort of gossip. Then one day the minister and deacon call at his house and ask to speak with Charlotte. It flashes through his mind that the church is about to take action against her. This realization of the existence of a social order is his first step back into normal life. He orders Charlotte to go home, and she unwillingly does so. When she leaves, he once more brings his "terrible will" into play—this time to undo the damage it had previously done. If his volition had twisted his body, it could now straighten it. In physical agony he rises from his chair and forces himself to stand erect. Then he fights his way step by step to Charlotte's house. Finally, he "stood before them all with that noble bearing which comes from humility itself when it has fairly triumphed. . . . and Barney entered the house with his old sweetheart and his old self" (329–30).

It will always be a question whether Barnabas's change of heart is plausible. Each reader must decide, but one should recall certain facts. Barnabas does have an "old," that is, a different, self, which the reader glimpses vividly in chapter 1. He has walked out into a spring evening that is fragrant with apple blossoms and pellucid with the threat of frost, ominous perhaps, for the future. He is on his way to see Charlotte, and he stops for a moment at the nearly completed house where she will live with him: "The tears came into his eyes; he stepped forward, laid his smooth boyish cheek against a partition wall . . . , and kissed it. It was a fervent demonstration, not towards Charlotte alone, nor the joy to come to him within those walls, but to all life and love and nature, although he did not comprehend it" (7). Furthermore, Freeman does state that Barnabas's transformation is the result of a newly found humility. Now the compulsion that had caused him to reject Charlotte and board himself up in his unfinished house had originated with humiliated pride. Humiliation exacerbates pride and generates self-lacerating impulses—or at least so think Gide and Dostoyevski. The pattern is one already seen in Freeman's writing: humility, the negation of pride, releases one from the clutches of a perverted, self-destructive will. Humility itself is generated by selfless love. In her introduction, Freeman stated that *Pembroke* is designed to demonstrate that the diseased will can be cured only by love; and it was exactly at the point where Barnabas was able to care more about Charlotte's sacrifice of her good name than about his own wounded pride that he was able to redirect his will away from self and thus effect his bodily and spiritual cure.

It was been said that even the most distorted wills in Freeman's fiction exert themselves in accomplishing what their possessors think is right. I believe this is an erroneous generalization. Barnabas frequently realizes that what he is doing is wrong. At times he tries to make material restitution to Charlotte in the form of gifts (which she refuses), for he has become wealthy in his life of solitary and frenzied labor.

It is also possible for a will to be directed not only toward what one thinks is right but toward what is intrinsically right, as is the case with Charlotte. The night Barnabas quarrels with her father she follows her lover into the street and calls after him, even when her father orders her back. Though she feels the humiliation of rejection, she slowly recovers from it. No longer smarting from her own hurt, she is able to understand the structure of Barnabas's ailment and feel compassion for him. She goes to his house to try to reason with him, not abjectly, but to help him as well as herself. When she caresses him at the time of his mother's death and later when she nurses him in his illness, she dismisses the objections of her parents and their fears of what people will say with the simple assertion: "I am doing what I think is right" (324).

A Gallery of Grotesques—Deborah Thayer

To understand Barnabas thoroughly one must know his mother, Deborah Thayer, whose portrait is perhaps the most astonishing in this gallery of nineteenth-century Puritans. Deborah, aptly named after the warrior prophetess of the Old Testament, is presented through a remarkable series of similes, metaphors, and analogies. As she listened to her husband reading one of the imprecatory psalms, "her eyes gleamed with warlike energy . . . : she confused King David's enemies with those people who crossed her own will" (3). When she learned that her son Barnabas had jilted Charlotte, she was so outraged that she declared she would "be jest as hard on him as the Lord for it" (58). As Freeman explains, "Deborah never yielded to any of the vicissitudes of life; she met them in fair fight like enemies, and vanquished them, not with trumpet and spear, but with daily duties. It was a village story how Deborah Thayer cleaned all the windows in the house one afternoon when her first child had died in the morning" (95–96). When she and her son met after the break with Charlotte, "the two faces confronted each other in silence, while it was as if two wills clashed swords in advance of them" (103). In daily living, she spooned out gravy into a bowl "as if it were molten lead instead of milk; . . . she might . . . have been one of her female ancestors in the times of the French and Indian Wars, casting bullets with the yells of savages in her ears . . ." (146). She administered medicine in a spoon to her sick son Ephraim "as if it were a bayonet and there were death at the point" (221–22). When she learns how Ephraim died, "her face worked like the breaking up of an icy river" (247).

The fact is that Deborah at times confuses herself with God; always she is sure that her will is his. In her own household she is a despot, just as God, in her view, is a despot in his heaven. She has banished Barnabas, her equal in willpower, from the house. She opposes her daughter Rose's affair with a local boy until the girl becomes pregnant by him, is ordered from her home in a blizzard, and is married under duress to her lover in the home of the village whore, who alone among the townspeople has had the decency to take her in out of the snow. Most implacable is Deborah's domination over her younger son, Ephraim, a boy afflicted with serious heart disease. Deborah's theology is that of the Westminister Assembly of the mid-seventeenth century, the catechism of which was the basic document in New England Puritanism. Deborah accepts its Calvinistic doctrines without demur and regards herself as one of its faithful supporters and propagators. Ephraim is so ill that the doctor has forbidden him all boyish play and has cautioned against rich food and corporal punishment. Yet Deborah considers it her duty to drum the catechism mercilessly into him, despite his precarious health, for she believes the immortal soul is more important than the mortal body. Her duty, dictated directly by God, as she thinks, is to make Ephraim learn his catechism; and Ephraim does learn it, even to the extent of developing a conviction that he himself is one of the elect.

But for all the Lord's grace Ephraim is on the whole miserable. One day he rebels against God and his mother. He sneaks out of the house at night and joins another boy in coasting down a hill. Ephraim's release is a glorious one. He shouts deliriously as his sled races down the slope, and he beats his friend in speed and in distance. It is the one time in his life that he acts like a boy, and it is also the end of his life. The exertion and an entire mince pie that he had stolen from the larder the same night and consumed combine to given him his death sickness. Moreover, his mother, who does not yet know of the sledding party, whips him for another offense, against the physician's orders. She thinks the punishment necessary if the child's soul is to be saved: "It was a high purpose to Deborah Thayer. She did not realize the part which her own human will had in it. . . . 'Ephraim,' said his mother, 'I have spared the rod with you all my life because you were sick. Your brother and your sister have both rebelled against the Lord and against me'" (239). As she applies the rod with vigor, Ephraim dies.

Even as he dies under the scourge of her hand and her will, she prays over his corpse "a strange prayer, full of remorse, of awful agony, of self-defense of her own act, and her own position as the vicar of God upon earth for her child" (240). She declares to Jehovah that she would have laid Ephraim on the altar as Abraham laid Isaac. She prays most of her waking hours for nearly a year: "Deborah had not the least doubt that she had killed her son . . ." (245). Her problem is to square her will with God's. Gossip becomes menacing. There is talk of the church's taking action against her. Then one day Ephraim's companion divulges the story of the clandestine sledding party. While thanking the Lord for letting her know that she perhaps had not killed her son, Deborah herself falls dead of heart failure.

As Ann Douglas Wood has pointed out, Deborah Thayer violates every preconception of motherhood generally held by sentimentalists in the Victorian age,[7] just as in Deborah's daughter Rose we have a negation of the sentimental heroine. In these and other characters Freeman has achieved a measure of realism opposed to the norm in popular fiction, at least, in her times. Yet there is another vein of realism, less shocking probably to Freeman's readers, in her depiction of the life of the village. Alongside its sordid aspects the village has its charms: the children celebrating May by picking wildflowers to present to their neighbors, the cherry-picking frolic—"a little bacchanalian rout in a New England field on a summer afternoon" (138)—and, throughout, brief descriptions of the landscape and weather in all seasons and glimpses of the farming and other daily activities of the community.

"Not a Summer Vacation"

Pembroke is Freeman's finest novel—one of the best novels thus far written on New England village life—and it won enthusiastic acclaim. Conan Doyle pronounced it the most impressive novel written in America since *The Scarlet Letter.*[8] Edwin Arlington Robinson, reading it in Gardiner, Maine, a town in which Freeman would have felt herself no stranger, declared that the book was true to New England as he knew it. His remarks in a letter to Harry DeForest Smith, written 28 October 1894, stand today as the novel's outstanding appreciation. To Robinson, *Pembroke* was

strange in its very simplicity. Everything is drawn against a tragic background of subdued passion and some of the scenes are almost magnificent in their treatment. To the careless reader the plot—or rather the plots—will seem impossible and contrary to human nature; but to one who knows anything about Puritanism the book will be interesting and impressive. Narrow-minded and unsympathetic readers had better keep away from it. It is a rather significant fact that it finds more appreciation in England than in America. . . .[9]

Robinson then says that he admires Freeman for "treating some things so openly." In referring to "a few animal touches that are hardly like anything else that I have ever seen in novels,"[10] he probably has in mind the events preceding Barnabas's sister's "shotgun" wedding—almost the norm in small New England villages during the past hundred years or so—and to the description of the village whore at whose house the wedding was performed. Robinson praises the style of the book as "eminently qualified for reading aloud. It never drags for a page and is always either bright or gloomy. Although it 'ends well' in a way, *Pembroke* life is not a summer vacation. It is pretty much like any other life,—that is, relatively."[11] In *Pembroke* Robinson was probably seeing much of his own town of Gardiner, where his life also was proving to be far from a summer vacation. His own first poems, soon to appear, dealing with Tilbury Town, as he called Gardiner, evoke the same somber background he finds in Freeman's novel. The "Satanic kinks"[12] that bedevil so many of the Tilbury citizens resemble the diseased wills of Freeman's characters. In both cases the defects, which exert a somewhat deterministic influence, are presented as inevitable outcroppings of the village environment and its moribund tradition.

Madelon

In Freeman's *Madelon,* published by Harper in 1896, the village of Ware Centre, Vermont, is the scene of a stabbing that almost takes a man's life. The assailant is Madelon Hautville, a high-spirited, dark-haired girl of French and Indian ancestry diluted by marriages for several generations into Yankee families. The victim is Lot Gordon, a sickly, bookish man hopelessly in love with Madelon. Madelon herself is in love with Lot's cousin Burr, who has jilted her for a golden-haired Anglo-Saxon girl, Dorothy Fair, daughter of the Orthodox Congregationalist parson. One night as Madelon is returning from a dance at which Burr has made evident his preference for Dorothy, Lot in desperation accosts her on the dark woods road and attempts to kiss her. Mistaking him for his cousin, she stabs him with a knife that her brother Richard has lent her to drive off bears. Lot falls, badly hurt but not dead. Running back to the village for help, Madelon meets Burr, tells him what has happened, and takes him back to the wounded man. Other merrymakers from the dance approach along the road. Burr successfully urges Madelon to return home. He remains behind. Richard, who has been following his sister to make sure she gets home safely, comes up; Burr Gordon gives him back his bloody knife, first wiping it on the snow. Burr then lays down his own knife in the pool of blood from Lot's wound. The merrymakers arrive on the scene, and Burr is incriminated beyond all reasonable doubt. He is arrested and placed in the county jail.

Madelon confesses to the assault, but no one believes her. It has been pointed out that her position is somewhat like Raskolnikov's, who is not believed when he confesses to murder. Freeman in fact had recently read *Crime and Punishment,* of which she said: "I am at odds with the whole thing, but it is a wonderful book. [Dostoyevski] writes with more concentrated force than Tolstoi. This book seems to me like one of my own nightmares, and told on my nerves."[13] But the resemblance between *Madelon* and *Crime and Punishment* is slight. Madelon has committed a crime of passion, not one of intellectual premeditation like

Raskolnikov's. Nor does Madelon attempt to conceal her guilt. From the beginning she is bent on confession; and when she learns that Burr, whom she still loves, is in jail for her crime, she becomes "nothing but a purpose concentrated on one end; there was in her that great impetus of the human will which is above all the swift forces of the world when once it is aroused."[14] Her purpose, of course, is to free Burr from the consequences of the crime that she committed.

Madelon, then, is another of Freeman's explorations of the potentialities of the will. Madelon herself is presented as a combination of passion stemming from her Indian forebears and of Calvinistic conscience and pertinacity traceable to the New England strain in her heritage. She has all the sense of duty, the single-mindedness of Freeman's most willful characters. She differs from a "pure-blooded" New Englander only in her fiery temperament, which Freeman associated with dark-haired Indians and the French rather than with fair-haired Anglo-Saxons. Madelon is thus an example of the dark heroine whose malignity, as Harry Levin has pointed out,[15] was so commonly contrasted in nineteenth-century fiction with the benignity of blue-eyed blondes, for example, in Hawthorne's *The Blithedale Romance* and Melville's *Pierre.* But Madelon is a member of Parson Fair's Congregational church and has a mother and grandmother of English descent. The passion attributed to the "darkness" of her foreign blood when tempered with English restraint and Calvinistic theology produces a thrust of purpose not to be resisted. Poor Dorothy Fair, daughter of the Puritans though she is, is passive in contrast, despite the fact she has the strength of will to defy her father and refuse to marry Burr.

Madelon is not successfully characterized. The explanation of her behavior in terms of her heredity is unconvincing and unnecessary. Girls of Anglo-Saxon stock elsewhere in Freeman's work display powers of will equal to those of Madelon and an equal propensity for holding themselves "to duty, like a knife to a grindstone" (248), and for equally passionate outbursts of emotion. Madelon is most credible when Freeman forgets her lineage and presents her simply as a village girl of strong feelings in a situation that challenges human capacities to the utmost. When Madelon walks ten miles to the county jail in the coldest weather within living memory in an attempt to free her lover of the charge of murder, she takes on a heroic stature that she lacks elsewhere; for she is here presented not as a combination of hereditary forces but only as a woman of strong conscience and a sense of duty, and with a lover's selflessness. The irrelevant ramifications of her family tree no longer obtrude.

The reader's impression of Madelon's passion, moreover, is enhanced by "the terrible rigor and tension of the cold" (144), which has shut down on the lonely terrain and the little lost villages like a granite lid, threatening to stifle the breath of life of all who venture from their hearths. Indeed, Freeman's outstanding achievement in the book is her evocation of the starkness of the long Vermont winter in which most of the action occurs: the terror of a subzero night when house timbers creak and crack as much from the cold as from the battering northwester, the two-day blizzard with its aftermath of gales that move the snow "across the fields in great diamond-glittering shafts" (201), the sudden thaw—like the melting of the congealed wills of some of her characters—when the air is "full of the sounds of running water, of sweet interrupted tinkles and sudden gurgles and steady outpourings as from a thousand pitchers" (229).

With equal success Freeman sketches in the background of village society, "sunken in the monotony and isolation of a Vermont country winter" (173). But the gossip, suspicion, and meddlesomeness are not seasonal; for Ware Centre, summer and winter, is not far removed in spirit from witch-hunting Salem: "That black atmosphere of suspicion and hatred, which gathers nowhere more easily than in a New England town, was thick around Burr and Madelon. They breathed, though as yet it was in less degree, the same noxious air as did the persecuted Quakers and witches of bygone times" (334). Later suspicion and hatred give rise to the spirit of "righteous retribution which finds easy birth in New England villages" (358), and threats are made against the persons of Madelon and Burr. In her depiction of the townspeople as a group, Freeman betrays her own conviction of something very like original sin: "The gases which lie at the bottom of human souls, which gossip and suspicious imaginations upstir, are deadlier than those at the bottom of old wells " (334). The human mind, she believes, has a tendency "born of involuntary self-knowledge which leads it to suspect a selfish motive in all untoward actions" (207).

Among the characters other than Madelon, Burr Gordon is the most interesting because of the conversionlike change of heart that he undergoes. Much of the action of the book rises from the fact that Burr is actually in love with two women—the dark-haired Madelon and the golden-haired Dorothy Fair. Perhaps Freeman intended an allegory on two aspects of women that attract men—mysterious, sometimes destructive passionateness; and open, innocuous prettiness. Burr is torn between the two Ware Centre girls. The final and conclusive weighting of Burr's love toward Madelon occurs in church the Sunday after he has been jilted at his wedding by the timorous Dorothy.

Burr had been willing to shoulder the blame for Lot's stabbing in order to save Madelon. Yet he had been ready enough to marry Dorothy; according to Freeman man loves woman rather than a particular individual woman. Now in church Burr listens to Madelon while she sings "the old orthodox hymns" (317) with all the beauty of her superb voice. Though the novel abounds in sentimental passages, this is not one of them. Burr and Madelon are no more than conventionally religious; they are not in the least pious or sanctimonious. Yet important in their lives has been Parson Fair's church, which both attend regularly and in which Madelon sings in the choir. The change in Burr is not a religious conversion, but it is the psychological equivalent of one. Madelon's voice and the words and notes of the old hymns release the "love and force which are at the roots of things for the strengthening of the world. . . . When Madelon Hautville stopped singing not one in the meeting-house had seen Burr Gordon stir, but the soul in him had surely turned and faced about with a great rending as of swathing wills that bound it" (317–18).

The Chain of Self-Sacrifice

The strong point of *Madelon* is descriptive accuracy. It has interest and value as a study of New England village life; as a novel it is not a success, and Freeman knew it. One weakness was her attempt in the narrative sections—not in the descriptive ones—to write in a style totally different from her usual naturalness and simplicity. Stilted inversions of normal English word order abound, and there are occasional archaisms. (Fortunately Freeman soon abandoned her experimentation with this pseudoromantic affectation and returned to her own more natural style.) A greater weakness of *Madelon* results from Freeman's trying to cram too much between two covers: realistic reporting on village life, several romantic love affairs, and considerable physical violence. She injected the violence, perhaps, because of the success she had achieved with a detective story, based loosely on the Lizzie Borden murder case, "The Long Arm," which she had written in 1895 in collaboration with J. E. Chamberlin, a columnist for the *Boston Evening Transcript,* and which won a $2,000 prize from the Bacheller Syndicate. If violence was so rewarding in one story, why not try it in another?

Freeman's handling of the romantic and sentimental love motif in

Madelon is at best regrettable. As she had already demonstrated in scores of short stories and novels, courtship and marriage in New England villages are not carried on according to the formulas of the standard popular fiction of the day, in which self-sacrifice ran rampant. William Dean Howells in *The Rise of Silas Lapham* (1885) had ridiculed plots in which self-sacrifice is a ruling yet totally unrealistic source of motivation among fictional characters. It is exactly this brand of sentimentality that Freeman has chosen to impose on her story of Ware Centre, Vermont. Self-sacrifice is the order of the day. Burr attempts to sacrifice his life by assuming the blame for the stabbing of Lot, who for a time is expected to die from the wound. Second, Lot, by swearing that his injury is the result of attempted suicide, sacrifices his reputation to free Burr in order to please Madelon. In return for this act, he exacts a promise from Madelon that she will marry him; but he later self-sacrificially releases her from the promise so that she can marry as she wishes. In the meanwhile, Madelon sacrifices herself by insisting that Burr marry Dorothy Fair; and Eugene Hautville, one of Madelon's brothers, who also loves Dorothy, sacrifices his feelings so that she can marry Burr, whom he hates. Only Dorothy's brainless fear that Burr actually is a murderer causes her not to go through with the marriage, and thus the chain of self-sacrifice is broken and the weddings which should have occurred long ago are finally celebrated. Even for a nineteenth-century readership, this fare apparently was too heady, for the book was poorly received.

Chapter Six
Beyond Local Color

Anthologists and literary historians frequently classify Freeman as a local colorist. Yet local color is so vague a term as to be without significant meaning. Hamlin Garland reduced the concept to absurdity when he included in it any literary work that conveys a feeling for a place or a period of time.[1] Thus Dickens, whose novels convey vivid impressions of London and rural England in his day, would qualify as a local colorist, as would Chaucer with his vignettes of medieval England. The *Iliad,* too, would qualify, since Homer's description of Achilles' shield portrays aspects of daily life in ancient Greece.

"I didn't even know I was a realist"

Freeman herself was puzzled not only by the term *local color* but by other equally vague literary terms, such as *realism* and *romanticism*. On the occasion in 1926 of her receiving the William Dean Howells Gold Medal for Fiction from the American Academy of Letters, she alluded to criticism of herself and others for "making too much use of [local color], for placing too much stress upon backgrounds of limited areas." Freeman's defense was that in a country as vast as the United States "in area and composition" one cannot set "one little work of fiction . . . against the whole. . . . One really has to go, as it were, into a room of this Country in order to have one's work visible." In words reminiscent of Hawthorne and Henry James in their complaints about the paucity of material for the novelist in America, she points to the nation's lack of a unifying historical background.[2]

Freeman, when asked what authors had influenced her, answered that none had. She had read extensively Dickens, Thackeray, Emerson, Jewett, Whittier, Tolstoi, Hardy, and many others. Significantly, she denied having read Jane Austen, with whom she was frequently compared. Concerning her own writing, she informed Pattee, "I sat down and wrote my little stories about the types I knew, they sold. That is really all."[3] She was equally firm in denying that she was consciously practicing literary realism, which under the sponsorship of Howells and others had become fashionable in the late nineteenth century and which, according to some critics, her writing exemplified. "I didn't even know that I'm a realist until they wrote and told me," she remarked in 1890.[4] To Garland she disclaimed knowing that realism was in vogue and insisted that even if she had known, she could not have intentionally set about being a realist,[5] and she protested that she had merely written about what she knew best and that her aim had been to make the people in her fiction true to life as to their personal traits, their actions, and their speech.[6] She repeated these thoughts later in response to queries made by Pattee and in advice she gave to would-be woman writers.[7]

Freeman did admit to Garland that she might "be a realist in spite of myself" because she lived and wrote "in a realistic age."[8] And the fact is, she does contribute importantly to a contemporary literary trend that was especially strong in New England. Irving, Cooper, Hawthorne, Longfellow, and Whittier earlier in the century had concentrated on the scenery, the people, and the history of their regions in an effort to find material suitable for a genuinely American literature. Even earlier, rural New England—Freeman's source for most of her writing—had aroused interest as presented by Timothy Dwight (1752–1817) in his *Travels in New England and New York* (1821–22), Catharine Sedgwick in *A New-England Tale* (1822), and John Carver (pen-name for Nathaniel S. Dodge) in *Sketches of New England* (1842)— all of which focused on the way of life in the New England countryside. Continuing in much the same vein was Whittier, who had high praise later for Freeman's work. A Massachusetts farmer's son, Whittier, who involved himself deeply in the abolitionist movement, was happiest when he could forget politics and write poetry and prose about past and present life in New England, especially as lived on the farms and in the villages.

Much of Whittier's writing is romantic, as in the idyllic "Snow-Bound" (1866), which idealizes life on a farm. But his stated goal, nevertheless, was to write truthfully about the rural folks he had known from childhood. Thus he praised the writings of an obscure Scottish dialect poet, Robert Dinsmore, long resident in New Hampshire, whose poems contained "no euphuism or transcendentalism,— the plainer and commoner the better. . . . Never having seen a nightingale, he makes no attempt to describe the fowl; but he has seen the night-hawk, at sunset, cutting the air above him, and he tells of it.

Side by side with his waving corn-fields and orchard-blooms we have the barn-yard and pigsty."[9] Whittier himself, accordingly, in the prelude to his long poem "Among the Hills" (1869) gives an unrelenting account of rural squalor and meanness blighting a beautiful natural scene. In the second half of the century a number of authors, including Harriet Beecher Stowe, Sarah Orne Jewett, Rose Terry Cooke, and Elizabeth Stuart Phelps Ward, produced fiction that convincingly recorded in its favorable and unfavorable aspects life outside the larger cities of New England. In the background was Ralph Waldo Emerson, whose "The American Scholar" (1837) had urged authors to use American materials and to concentrate on the common rather than the unusual or sensational aspects of life. Following Emerson, Thomas Wentworth Higginson made much the same plea in an *Atlantic Monthly* essay, "Americanism in Literature" (January 1870). The cry on all sides was for writers to write honestly and truthfully about what they knew at firsthand—that is, do precisely what Freeman described herself as doing. It is interesting that she knew Higginson's sister in Brattleboro and had heard Higginson lecture there.

Moral Earnestness

But Emerson and Higginson demanded that American literature be imbued with moral earnestness— a demand that hardly needed to be made for New England authors. Cooke, Jewett, Ward, and Freeman all made clear moral statements in most of their writing. Jewett, in a preface to *Deephaven* (1877), insisted that her purpose was to make known to the rest of the world the dignity of the Maine people about whom she was writing. Ward, a sterner moralist, in her autobiographical *Chapters from a Life* (1896) titled one of her chapters "Art for Truth's Sake," and in it she argued that "the province of the artist is to portray life as it is; and life *is* moral responsibility." Hence a realistic author must be concerned with morals, though the moral of a literary production must not be too obviously "pointed."[10] It is clear to any reader that Freeman was concerned with morals, or "moral responsibility," but that she abstains from obtrusively pointing the intrinsic morals of her writings.

Freeman, then, was writing in a climate that might be described as one of limited realism—a realism sponsored by Howells through the nation's two most prestigious periodicals, the *Atlantic Monthly* and *Harper's New Monthly*. But we must accept Freeman's word that she was not influenced by other writers. The evidence bears her out. Her style, psychological insights, and ironic humor all set her apart from her contemporary New England authors. But granting all this, one must accept the fact, as did Freeman, that she was a leading figure in a literary movement that might be described as realistic regionalism. Willy-nilly, she was caught up in the literary zeitgeist. That she was entirely unaware of this zeitgeist is improbable. She was acquainted with the work of most, if not all, authors discussed here. Some she states that she has read and admired (Jewett, for example); all of them wrote for periodicals that Freeman read and in some cases wrote for. Furthermore Freeman was pliant to editorial demands—with some editors she was on very friendly terms—and these demands reflected the reading tastes and trends of the times, which in turn the editors themselves were instrumental in forming.

"Not the best work of which I am capable"

Freeman, indeed, bluntly stated that she wrote for the market, because her motive was money. In "The Girl Who Wants to Write" she stated: "The feeling that one 'must write' is . . . a doubtful proposition. It is, I conclude, supposed to argue such inspiration, such seething of central fires of genius, that expression or disaster must ensue. In reality . . . a woman may write something for money with which to buy a French hat."[11] At least until her marriage Freeman herself depended on her writing for support of herself and an indigent aunt. After her marriage the proceeds from her writing went in part for self-indulgences; for example, the $20,000 earned by *The Shoulders of Atlas* (1908) paid for a new house in Metuchen. Thus regarding her writing most importantly as a source of income, Freeman tried her hand at many branches of her craft. She had begun in 1880 with poetry and short tales for children, but soon started writing for adults as well; within ten years she added novels to her repertoire; next she had a fling at playwriting and even worked on several movie scenarios. Writing was her trade and she was versatile at it.

Yet Freeman was dissatisfied with her writings, and she complained to Pattee: "My accomplished work is not the best work of which I am capable. . . ."[12] Nor was it even the kind of writing that she would have liked to have done. "I want more symbolism, more mysticism," she informed Pattee. "I left that out because it struck me people did not want it, and I was forced to consider selling qualities. Of course I tried to make my work good along its own lines."[13] Nevertheless, especially as her reputation became established and her self-confidence grew, she did indulge her penchant for symbolism, as for example in "A New England Nun"; and later mysticism appeared in stories in *Six Trees* (1903), *Understudies* (1903), and elsewhere. Nor did her sales decline as a result.

Freeman's prodigious literary output—thirty volumes for adult readers, not to mention her writing for children and many uncollected periodical pieces—was achieved with some sacrifice of quality, particularly during the Metuchen years. Still, even as late as 1914 she was capable of writing an occasional story that equaled her very finest.

Freeman's Comments on Emily Brontë

Freeman's comments on the works of other authors are rare even in her personal letters. She does, as already mentioned, list some of the writers whom she has read—disclaiming their influence on her; but she does not discuss them. One exception is a brief essay, "Emily Brontë and *Wuthering Heights*," which she contributed to a volume entitled *The World's Great Women Novelists* (1901). The essay is interesting not only for what Freeman says about Brontë but also for what she says about women as authors. She begins by stating that "there are certainly forces at work in *Wuthering Heights* beyond those" in the novels of Emily's sister Charlotte Brontë: "While the book is offensive, even repulsive, it has the repulsiveness of power. Charlotte Brontë's books are unmistakably those of a woman—a woman fretting at and scorning the limitations of her sex and her day, yet in a measure yielding to them. But Emily . . . overleaps the barriers" and ignores her own and her readers' sensibilities. Her purpose was to write the truth about her characters, and as a result she "handles brutality and coarseness as another woman would handle a painted fan."[14] One calls to mind Freeman's complaint that in her own writing she had to settle for something less than truth in order to satisfy her editors and not offend her readers. In other words, she was under the handicap of having to write in a manner that custom considered appropriate for a woman writing mainly for other women. But in *Wuthering Heights* "there is evident no quiver of feminine nerves in the mind or hand."[15]

Freeman, indeed, marvels that *Wuthering Heights* could have been written by a woman, especially a woman so isolated from the world as were the Brontë sisters. How, she asks, did Emily gain her understanding of "the primitive brutalities and passions, and the great truth of life that sanctifies them . . ."? As for the love of Heathcliff and Catherine, Freeman finds that, despite its adulterous nature, "it gives . . . a sense of innocence and stern purity. . . ." Only a woman writer, "perhaps only a maiden woman could portray a scene of such passion and innocence" as that between the dying Catherine and Heathcliff; for "perhaps only a woman could have in her brain the conception of such forces and not make them a part of her own life."[16] Yet she insists that Emily's personality does not obtrude into the novel, and she warns that one should be wary of judging an author by her or his writings.

Of the greatness of *Wuthering Heights* Freeman has no doubts. One wonders, moreover, how much the example of this novel may have contributed to the characterization of Madelon, whose passion and potential for violence make her a sort of female Heathcliff. Further, the wintry Vermont countryside so prominent in *Madelon* rivals Brontë's Yorkshire moors in wild bleakness. But above all, Freeman's essay reveals in her an awareness of the role of sexuality in human affairs that is not so evident in most of her other writing, partly because of editorial requirements, no doubt, and partly because in the men and women in her fiction sexuality had often been suppressed into dormancy.

Chapter Seven

God's Paupers and Man's: Two Studies in Poverty

Jerome, A Poor Man: Plot and Setting

Freeman's next novel after *Madelon* marks a shift from a primary interest in the conscience and the will to a concern with the psychological effects of poverty, the chief social and economic problem in the New England of her day. The shift is indicated in the subtitle of the book, *Jerome, A Poor Man,* published in 1897. Her longest novel to date— over five hundred pages—it was not her best in technique or style, though it was an improvement on *Madelon.* Among its drawbacks is its length—the result of an inordinately protracted pair of love complications, the untangling of which requires half the book. In addition, the plot depends on several gimmicks that stretch the reader's powers of belief beyond the breaking point.

The action is set in motion by the disappearance, interpreted as suicide, of the twelve-year-old Jerome's father, who had been fighting a losing battle against poverty that would become total destitution upon the imminent foreclosure of the mortgage on his farm. Despite the absence of a corpse, a funeral is held; and then the family sets about the task of survival without him. At the end, however, Abel Edwards, the father, reappears, a broken old man. All the time, he divulges, he had been working on a farm twenty miles away, amassing the money to pay the mortgage. Very likely Freeman had in mind Hawthorne's "Wakefield," the story of a man who on a whim vanishes from his wife in London by merely moving into the next street but returns to her, again on a whim, after a lapse of twenty years. But the New England countryside, where communities are connected with one another by a network of friends and kin, is not so favorable as London for this kind of anonymity.

Another device upon which the plot hinges is an agreement signed by Jerome and two grasping moneylenders in the town, Simon Basset and Dr. Prescott, to the effect that if the poverty-stricken Jerome ever received $25,000 and distributed the sum among the poor, the other two would distribute in a like manner one quarter of their fortunes.

The village of Upham, in which the novel is laid, is the most completely described of Freeman's fictional communities, possibly excepting Pembroke. It is clearly a Vermont village, for some of the landmarks of the Brattleboro vicinity appear in it; and one of the most melodramatic events in the novel, the flooding of Greystone Brook, which destroys Jerome's sawmill, recalls a destructive flooding of Whitestone Brook in Brattleboro, an event Freeman had witnessed as a girl. But Upham suggests Vermont of the 1880s and 1890s in more basic ways. The fearful poverty in it among all but a few of the gentry was the condition in most hill towns. Freeman shows all levels and gradations of this poverty, beginning with an appalling view of the poorhouse with its population of idiots, paupers, orphans, crones, and persons only temporarily "on the town." The poorhouse is symbolically situated close to the village, for most of the townspeople are never far from destitution. Outside the poorhouse by dint of desperate and ceaseless struggle are the majority of the citizens, represented by the Edwardses and the Uphams, who cultivate pitiably small and sterile farms burdened by mortgages always on the verge of foreclosure; by the Judds and the Lambs, who eke out a living by sewing shoes for a local entrepreneur; and by several shopkeepers not notably more prosperous than their customers. The comparative well-being of the gentlefolk and professional people, such as Lawyer Means, Dr. Prescott, Squire Merrit, and Colonel Lamson, serves only to accentuate the misery of the others.

The Pride of the Poor

The bitterness of rural poverty was the subject of other writers in Freeman's day, for example, of Edgar Watson Howe and Hamlin Garland. Freeman's originality lies in her analysis of the psychological impact of pauperism. Poverty, she perceived, constitutes a humiliation, especially in communities with a heritage of Calvinism, which tended to regard one's worldly state as an indication of one's standing with God. Humiliation, she further understood, has the effect of enhancing pride. She knew, perhaps from the experience of poverty or near-poverty in her own family, that poor people are often excessively proud and that their pride, sharpened by their misfortunes, expresses itself in irrational acts of harm to themselves or others. As an example, in *Jerome*

Adoniram Judd's family, kin to the Edwardses, lives with one foot in the poorhouse. The Judd dwelling is mortgaged, the son is blind, work is scarce. The son's blindness can be cured if money can be found to send him to Boston for an operation. Jerome, who has been saving to buy a sawmill, offers the money, but Mrs. Judd refuses to take it. To accept money, she asserts, would be worse than letting her son remain blind: "Nobody shall sacrifice himself for my son. If our own prayers and sacrifices are not sufficient, it is the will of the Lord that he should suffer, and he will suffer."[1] More important to her than her son's eyesight is her honor, her determination to be self-sufficient.

And Mrs. Judd is consistent in her refusal to accept help. When Jerome unexpectedly inherits $25,000 from Colonel Lamson, he divides the sum among the one hundred poorest people in the town in accord with the agreement he had made on a dare some years before. The Judds are thus eligible to receive $250. Moreover, Dr. Prescott, who is party to the agreement, decides to write off a number of mortgages, one of them on the Judd homestead. Mrs. Judd's refusal of both offers is notable for its emotion rather than its logic: "I sha'n't take money that's given in any such way, and neither will my son. . . . We sha'n't take what Dr. Prescott has offered neither—to give us the mortgage on our house. It's an honest debt, and we don't want to shirk it. If we're paupers, we'll be paupers of God, but of no man!" (482).

A similar pride is the foundation of Jerome's character, which is one of the most convincingly and sympathetically delineated in all of Freeman's works. At the age of twelve Jerome had displayed his pride by refusing to accept some gingerbread from the Squire's daughter, Lucina, who will one day be his bride. But having rudely refused her gift, he insists on giving Lucina a piece of sassafras root that he has dug up in a swamp; and she, not being poor, has the grace to accept it. He comes by his pride in his home; his mother, a cripple, insists on sending to wealthy Mrs. Prescott her "china bowl with pink flowers on it" (14) full of parsnip soup in return for a pitcher of lamb broth that Mrs. Prescott had sent her. Though Mrs. Judd's children go hungry that evening, she has the satisfaction of saying: "Now I guess Mis' Doctor Prescott won't think we're starvin' to death here, even if her husband has got a mortgage on our house" (17).

Pride of Spirit

All through life Jerome is generous to a fault. As a boy, he gives his time and strength to his family, of which he is the sole support after the disappearance of his father. Later he learns something of medicine, the use of herbs and the diagnosis and treatment of the more common diseases, so that he can treat free of charge those who are too poor to pay Dr. Prescott's fees. Though working furiously to buy a sawmill, he freely offers his savings to any one in need; and later he apportions his unexpected inheritance among the village poor. Though the religious revivals that sometimes excited the town never brought him to conversion, he is convinced of God's justice and that his own duty is to "apply his small strength towards furthering what he could, if no more than an atom, of the eternal will . . ." (262). Clearly God's will is to help the poor.

When things go wrong for Jerome and he loses his mill in a flood, he regards his misfortune as "the whip-lash for sin" (454) that he might have committed. And when on receiving his inheritance, he is tempted to keep it for himself, contrary to his signed pledge, he ransacks his conscience with a skill that would do credit to the Mathers and which Freeman attributes to his "generations of Calvinistic ancestors" (465). But Jerome has his moments of mystical insight. Walking on a country road one spring at dusk, he had "a vague impression which he did not express to himself, that he had come to a door wide open into spaces beyond all needs and desires of the flesh and the earthly soul. . . . The image even of the beautiful Lucina . . . faded" (282).

But Jerome remains a victim of spiritual pride. He gives but he refuses to receive. When friends offer him help after the loss of his mill, he rejects aid as summarily as would the Judds. He will be God's pauper, not man's. Lucina, whom he loves and who is well-to-do, becomes physically ill because he will not marry her until he is wealthy enough to support her in her accustomed style of living. In this stubbornness he persists, though he believes love to be "the one truth and reality and source of all things" (497). Finally Lucina's mother confronts him: "You generous—you! . . . You are a miser of a false trait in your own character. . . . What are you that you should say, 'I will go through life, and I will give, and not take'? What are you . . . that you should be towards your fellow-creatures as a God, conferring everything, receiving nothing?'" (502).

At this moment Jerome undergoes a conversion, perhaps not one acceptable to the church deacons, but a true change of heart. Jerome does not associate his spiritual metamorphosis in any close way with religion, but Freeman does. The direction of a stubborn will is reversed by a supreme counteracting effort of the will. One assumes that Jerome's generosity, his compassion for the poor, will remain, but not as manifestations of pride. He is now truly one of God's elect rather than one of God's paupers.

Style

Though marred by a preposterous plot, *Jerome* is highly effective in style. In *Madelon,* we have seen, Freeman had blemished the simplicity and vividness of her early manner by attempting to complicate and vary her sentence structure with clumsy and artificial inversions of word order and by resorting to archaic diction, as in this: "Sorely afraid was Dorothy Fair, if the truth were told, to go with this passionate girl, who had declared to her face that she had done murder . . ." (96). In *Jerome* Freeman has not returned entirely to the simplicity of her short stories, which was effective in them but slightly palling in the novels *Jane Field* and *Pembroke.* Rather she has achieved a style that is natural but sufficiently involved for the complexity and length of the novel form. Her sentences are varied in structure but not artificially; her diction is concrete; her paragraphs, especially the descriptive ones, are adequately and rhythmically developed. Word pictures like those of the flooding of the millstream, Jerome's old white horse pulling a sleigh or a plough, the gatherings in the local store, the poorhouse and its inmates are beautifully done. In these and others—for example, her many depictions of interiors of dwellings of both the rich and the poor—is caught the very essence of village life.

The Portion of Labor

Jerome is a study in rural poverty of the kind that Freeman had observed in Vermont and in Randolph where, along with the decline of agriculture, the construction of shoe factories in nearby Brockton had destroyed the cottage industry of sewing shoes, as was the case in the fictional Upham. In *The Portion of Labor* (1901), which explores the plight of the poor in a sizable New England manufacturing city, Freeman reveals conditions that are no less depressing. Daily life among the millworkers consists of hard work, periods of bare subsistence alternating with near starvation, fear, bitterness, and despair. Focusing upon a respectable working family, the Brewsters, whose Yankee lineage is as pure as that of the haughtiest Boston Brahmin, Freeman depicts these conditions with painful vividness and passionate indignation. One critic has described *The Portion of Labor* as Freeman's "most ambitious and least successful novel."[2] This opinion is simply not correct. Like much of her longer fiction it has serious weaknesses, but it also has strengths. Most impressive among the latter is the verisimilitude with which she presents the drab, gray manufacturing town with its snow-clogged streets, its offensively garish shopping area, its clanging streetcars, and its population of Yankees, Irish, Swedes, and Slavs, all merged beneath the shadow of the monolithic mills into a uniformity that blots out racial, national, and even individual differences. Such depressing cities were, and are, realities of our civilization. An effective reproduction of their atmosphere—and Freeman has done no less—is a worthwhile literary achievement.

In her depiction of the workers themselves Freeman has been equally successful, except for her heroine, Ellen Brewster. All of the dozen or so mill hands who play appreciable roles in the novel come convincingly to life: stolid Andrew Brewster with his hereditary New England conscience that afflicts him cruelly when he invests and apparently loses his savings in Colorado mining stock; earthy, coarse-mouthed, highly sexed Eva Loud, who marries the equally earthy and unpredictable Jim Tenny and goes insane when he deserts her for a former sweetheart; the vacuous Sadie Peele, who opposes a strike by the workers because it will mean she cannot buy the near-seal cape she has set her heart on; the hot-headed Amos Lee, who shoots at Ellen Brewster as she is leading the strikers back to work but hits and almost kills one of the owners instead; the bluff and flirtatious Irish foreman Ed Flynn, with whom half the female operatives are in love and who finally, out of pity, marries the moronic Mamie Brady after she almost does away with herself with a dose of laudanum taken in despondency brought on by his indifference to her—these are outstanding characterizations.

Freeman's treatment of her heroine, the beautiful, brilliant, strong-willed, and idealistic Ellen Brewster, is another matter, however. Like Freeman herself as a child, Ellen is pampered and pretty and bent on getting her own way. She has been teased as teacher's "partial" at school but is the center of a small group of staunch friends because of her brightness and beauty. In her family, which like the Wilkinses is dominated by a strong-willed mother, Ellen is the center of attention. One critic has called Ellen tiresome; and she is tiresome, in the manner of the Puritans from whom she is descended. Hers is the tiresomeness of an overdeveloped sense of duty that drives her to turn down the offer of a local rich woman to put her through Vassar and that prompts her instead to take a job in the mill to help support a lunatic aunt in an asylum. It is the tiresomeness of a hypersensitive conscience that finds its expression in interminable agonizings as to whether loyalty to class and her love for a young factory owner are compatible. On the day of her graduation from high school as valedictorian, she delivers a fiery, revolutionary tirade against capitalism. The sweetness of her face prevents most of the audience, with their notions of what is appropriate for a female, from taking her seriously. But her words have their origin in a fierce pride of family and in a fanatical idealism, and one can admire their sincerity. Her occasional moments of religious insight, when she can stand outside herself and say to her soul, "This I will always remember,"[3] are moving in themselves and are evidence of a growing mysticism in Freeman's view of life.

Calvinistic Economics

Freeman's presentation of the factory owners and their families is unconvincing. She herself came from a working-class, though not mill-working, family. Her sympathies were with the workers, and her understanding of them was instinctive and profound. But the wealthy people in *The Portion of Labor* are not only unfeeling but wooden in characterization. Freeman tries to be fair to them, to present their point of view; but she fails to interest the reader in their problems. Despairing, perhaps, of understanding them herself, she constantly emphasizes the impossibility of bridging the gap between classes. Neither side in the industrial struggle, she reiterates, has the ability or the desire to understand the other's position.

At a time when writers like Howells, Henry George, and Edward Bellamy were flooding the book market with blueprints for social reform, Freeman had no suggestions for the betterment of the system. Her book is, in fact, infused with a Calvinistic fatalism that would be enraging to a reformer. She does not blame the poor for their plight, for she bypasses in this novel the Calvinist notion that the poor are suffering in payment for their own or Adam's sin. But she accepts their lot as inevitable, as part of God's way with the world. To her the portion of labor is not what Howells or Bellamy would have it be—a fair share of what it produces. Rather it is what the author of Ecclesiastes designates it to be: "I withheld not my heart from any joy, for my heart rejoiced in all my labor, and that was my portion of labor" (563; Eccles. 2:10).

That Freeman could solve, with apparent satisfaction to herself, the problems of labor by one rather cryptic biblical quotation is a measure of the religious orientation of her thinking. But her resort to the scriptural words is not blind. They come at the end of as naturalistic a description of the evils of unemployment, low wages, and capitalistic exploitation as the most convinced socialist could desire. And they are uttered by a person, Andrew Brewster, whose pride of self and family has been bruised every month of every year of a long life, who has more than once been reduced to tears by the brutality of the industrial system, and who has seen his daughter sacrifice her education, his wife take in sewing at coolie wages, his coal scuttle stand empty by a frigid stove, while he has begged for jobs shoveling snow to earn the price of a loaf of bread. To repeat, there is nothing sentimental or purblind in Freeman's picturing of the lives of the poor. Yet Andrew Brewster "seemed to see that labor is not alone for itself, not for what it accomplishes of the tasks of the world, not for its equivalent in silver and gold, not even for the end of human happiness and love, but for the growth in character of the laborer" (563).

To most readers Andrew's conclusion will be ludicrously inadequate. It harks back to the New England of John Winthrop and the Mathers: God has ordained that the lives of men and women on earth be hard, that they earn their bread by the sweat of their brow, that life is a proving ground for the next world. Some such realization prompts Ellen to call off the strike: "A fancy seized her that rebellion and resistance were hopeless, that . . . yielding to the onslaughts of fate [was] as inevitable as life itself, one of its conditions" (473). To Freeman, if the workers could keep their integrity, above all their self-respect, they would have won a spiritual battle, the only kind, apparently, that really counted in her thinking. The Brewsters prove themselves, despite their poverty, to be among the sanctified. Their chief reward in this world will be the knowledge that they were able to endure; in the next world, the reasonable expectation is that the rewards will be greater if not more tangible.

Freeman's views regarding the problems of labor were by no means unique. For example, Lucy Larcom (1824–93), herself an operative as a girl in the Lowell textile mills in the 1840s and later a professor of literature and a poet of some standing, wrote in her autobiographical *A New England Girlhood* (1889) that "we were taught to work almost as if it were a religion; to keep at work, expecting nothing else. It was our inheritance, handed down from the outcasts of Eden. And for us,

as for them, there was a blessing hidden in the curse."[4] In another
work, the book-length, blank-verse poem *An Idyl of Work* (1873), Larcom insisted on the dignity of all labor, rejected strikes by female
textile workers as being unladylike and as substituting one tyranny for
another. She also condemned communal schemes like that of Brook
Farm as being intolerably stultifying to individual liberty. Yet she insisted that

> nobody should moil
> Just to add wealth to men already rich.
> Only a drudge will toil on, with no hope
> Widening from well-paid labor.[5]

Similarly the New England novelist Elizabeth Stuart Phelps Ward
(1844–1911) in a powerful work of fiction, *The Silent Partner* (1871),
dealing with life, particularly that of women, in textile mills, arrives
at the conclusion that the hardships of labor can be endured, if not
solved, by the workers' recourse to religion. All three of these New
England authors, then, reduce the workers' problem to a spiritual one.
In other words, they approach the matter from the standpoint, only
slightly modified, of their Calvinist ancestors.

Chapter Eight
Excursions into the Past and Other Diversions

In the decade between the publication of *A New England Nun* (1891) and *The Portion of Labor* (1901) Freeman's major effort went into the five novels thus far discussed. She had become thoroughly professional, had no trouble finding a market for her product, and enjoyed an almost universally favorable press in both America and Great Britain. Her energies were seemingly limitless; in addition to the five big novels, she published during this decade two lesser novels, a play, and four volumes of short stories. Three of these works—the play, one collection of short fiction, and one novel—record excursions into history.

Giles Corey and Salem

From both of her parents Freeman was descended from early settlers in Salem, and one of her ancestors, Bray Wilkins, had been instrumental in getting his grandson hanged as a witch. Unlike Hawthorne, who seemed to have qualms of conscience about the part one of his forebears had in the persecution of witches, Freeman took on no burden of guilt for her ancestor's actions, but her interest in Salem and witchcraft was more than that of an objective historian. In 1892, exactly two hundred years after the Salem delusion, Freeman published a six-act tragedy, *Giles Corey, Yeoman,* whose title character is a man condemned to death by being crushed under a weight—because he would not testify at his own trial.

In Freeman's characterization of Corey and his wife and in the plot of her drama she gives evidence of a close acquaintance with Charles W. Upham's two-volume *Salem Witchcraft,* published in 1866. Moreover, from Upham's detailed description of Salem in the late seventeenth century she may have absorbed much that is intrinsic in her own descriptions of village life in New England in her fiction. In Salem were the same tyranny of gossip, the same grudges and pettinesses that turned neighbor against neighbor and family members against each other. Above all in Upham's book she saw in operation, in its very worst aspects, the Puritanism that, somewhat mellowed and much less virulent, still lingered in the villages in her stories. Freeman's debt to Upham seems to have been considerable.

As presented by Upham, Corey, who was the father of four married daughters by the first of his three wives, was a strong-willed, rather rough man and was often the object of unfavorable gossip. He had been accused of arson and murder, but had been acquitted in both cases. He was a drinker, quick to use his fists, and cared little for public opinion. At the age of eighty he underwent religious conversion and, at the beginning of the witch scare, was admitted to full church membership. Now one of the Puritan saints, he could do no less than support the church in its battle against Satan's minions. He attended the trials. In his zeal he reported things about his wife that suggested witchcraft, and eventually she was tried and hanged. This woman, who was almost unique in Salem in that she denied the existence of witches there, figures importantly and sympathetically in the play, especially in the trial scene.

Just three days before his wife's execution, however, Giles Corey was "pressed" to death as required by English law for one who remained "mute." One motive for his stance was to save for his heirs his property, which would have been confiscated had he been convicted of witchcraft. Another motive attributed to him by both Upham and Freeman was to bear witness to his abhorrence of the persecutions and his own part in them. About to submit to his ordeal, he says to his daughter, who is pleading with him to give in to the court: "There be that which is beyond human ties to force a man, there be that which is at the root of things."[1] Giles is thus another of Freeman's iron-willed, stubborn New England villagers, but in this case one who is motivated, at least in part, by an ideal.

Giles Corey, Freeman's only drama of consequence, was not successful on the stage in either Boston or New York, but it attracted favorable attention as closet drama when published in *Harper's* in 1892 and as a book a year later. Freeman had adhered fairly closely to historical fact in the play, but she had weakened the overall effect by introducing a fictitious love motif and by introducing into the dialogue archaisms like "I trow" and "an you say so," which the remarkably unarchaic

English of the court records does not justify. Perhaps the chief value of
the play is the witness it bears to Freeman's interest in the Puritan past
of New England.

Silence and Other Stories

Silence and Other Stories (1898) is a volume of six short tales, all but
one of which are laid in the past of New England. The title piece deals
with the Deerfield Massacre of 1704. The plot, hinging on sentimental
love, need not concern us. But the presentation of life in a frontier
settlement, the unfailing wills and optimism of the people in the face
of frightful hardship, testify to the author's admiration for the older
Puritans, whose stubborn purposefulness served a worthwhile end and
was not expended on petty feuds and personal crotchets as in the decaying culture of her own times. Several of the lesser characters—for
example, the indomitable Widow Eunice Bishop, whose needles clash
like swords as she knits—are amusingly drawn.

The strongest of the stories in the collection is "A New England
Prophet," which relates an incident suggested by the Millerite hysteria
of the 1840s. Like the historical William Miller, the prophet in the
story has convinced himself and his followers that the world will end
on a certain day. At the appointed time, the band of believers, dressed
in flowing gowns of muslin, marches up a hill to await the end, only
to march down again when the dawn arrives as usual. During the night
the prophet's daughter, torn between loyalty to him and love for a
young man, has yielded to the latter and been married to him. The
message is obvious.

In this story are all the ingredients of Freeman's strongest fiction:
the fanatical prophet, fierce, unyielding, and humorless in his irrational conviction; the eruption of violent emotion among his following
of hitherto repressed farmfolk and villagers; the reversion to normalcy
at the end. The prophet, like Miller himself, is one of a long line of
visionaries beginning in the extreme Protestantism of Old England and
including in New England such zealots as Anne Hutchinson, many
leaders of the Great Awakening, and William Lloyd Garrison. No one
was more aware than Freeman of the explosiveness of the New England
character, which might be manifested in some personal reprisal, as in
"A Village Singer," or in a religious upheaval of great magnitude. In
"A New England Prophet" this potential of the Yankee character for
violent tangential action is exhibited vividly. The Prophet, whose fa-

naticism dehumanizes him, brings to mind similar obsessed and dehumanized characters in the tales and novels of Hawthorne.

The one story in *Silence* that Freeman laid in the present, "Evelina's Garden" (which was also published separately as a little book in 1899), deserves mention, for it was one of her favorites. It also invites comparison with Hawthorne. As in "Rappaccini's Daughter," a garden takes precedence, in a warped mind, over humanity and its happiness. Living in complete isolation from her fellow beings, Evelina, who is of a lineage superior to that of the other townspeople, devotes herself entirely to the cultivation of flowers. She has been frustrated in love, to be sure, but the frustration is the result of her family pride, which renders her incapable of letting her lover, of lower social station, know even by a glance that she returns his feelings for her. So she rejects humanity for flowers, even ceasing to attend church. In her will she demonstrates the seemingly total dehumanization of her heart by leaving to a relative, also named Evelina, her very substantial fortune under the provisos that she never marry and that she devote her life to the garden.

There has been an understanding between the local minister and the younger Evelina that they will eventually marry, but the minister now breaks the engagement from an excessive sense of duty—so excessive, in fact, that it is as dehumanizing as the elder Evelina's floral obsession. The minister, who is an embodiment of overly conscientious scruples rather than a man, rejects the many overtures of the girl, who is more than willing to give up her fortune. The minister's scruple, of course, is that he thinks it would be wrong of him to cause Evelina the loss of her inheritance by marrying her. When Evelina learns this, she sprinkles the flowers with boiling brine, thereby losing the inheritance; and the minister in a burst of penitent gratitude marries her.

Up to this point Freeman had written with a firm hand a story of twofold dehumanization overcome by young love. Unfortunately, she insisted on going one step further by passing off the eccentric will as being merely a means of testing the love of Evelina for the minister, who turns out to be the beneficiary in the event that Evelina mistreats the flowers.

The Heart's Highway

Silence and Other Stories was mainly historical fiction. In 1900 Freeman again returned to the historical genre with a novel of colonial

Tidewater Virginia, *The Heart's Highway*. Her acquaintance with the Tidewater arose from extensive sojourns at Old Point Comfort, where she found relief from the protracted disappointments of New England spring weather. Her motive for writing the book, apart from cashing in on the popularity of historical fiction, has been described as the urge "to satisfy a craving for the frankly beautiful and romantic. . . ."[2] If this is the case, she cannot be accused of curbing her appetite. The beauty of the flowering days and scented nights of the May countryside caresses her pages like a benediction. The excitement of intrigue and open rebellion spurred by Nathaniel Bacon carries the reader along surely and swiftly. The story, centered on the passionate love between Harry Wingfield and the willful, beautiful rebel Mary Cavendish, imparts to eros the ultimate of glamor. The triumphant closing sentence in the book, as spoken by the first-person narrator, reads: "For I have learned that the blazon of love is the only one which holds good forever through all the wilderness of history, and the path of love is the only one which those that may come after us can safely follow unto the end of the world."[3]

The love celebrated in *The Heart's Highway* is indeed solely eros, unleavened by agape, untrammeled by religious scruples, and only insignificantly impeded by social convention. The hero and heroine, of course, remain chaste, while unwedded, for the novel was written in 1900. But the depiction of the Barry brothers living unmarried on their plantation with their magnificently carnal black mistresses who carouse with their masters and their guests (and the guests' equally carnal white wives) provides a spectacle of unrestraint remarkable from the pen of an author who had hitherto confined herself, except in *Madelon,* to accounts of the chilly amours of latter-day Puritans. One suspects that in the imagined freedom of bygone Cavalier society Freeman was finding a relief from the frozen norm of New England morality. Her main impulse, rather than to write of the beautiful and the romantic, was very likely to write of the free and the uninhibited. Here was a society where the parson could frequent the taverns and gamble and race his horses and attend the carousings of the Barry brothers without being waited on by a committee of long-faced elders suggesting he submit his resignation. Thus in most ways *The Heart's Highway* marked a new departure for Freeman; and though it was well received by the general public, some readers were indignant that Freeman had deviated from her usual New England themes.

The Love of Parson Lord and Other Stories

Other ventures of Freeman into historical fiction were two preposterous stories in a generally very inferior collection entitled *The Love of Parson Lord and Other Stories* published in 1900. One of these, "The Tree of Knowledge," introduces cloak-and-dagger romance into the New England countryside of apparently the early nineteenth century. Even more ludicrous is "Catherine Carr," a tale of split loyalties during the War of 1812. One other piece in the volume—not in the historical genre—deserves some mention. In the title story, Parson Lord has promised God that his two daughters will be missionaries. His wife and elder daughter die, leaving him with the younger daughter, Love. The minister is now drawn between tenderness for his surviving child, whose sensitivity and fragile health hardly fit her for missionary work, and his covenant with God. He finds a legalistic solution to his dilemma: he refuses to marry his daughter to her lover, but he permits the local justice of the peace to do it. Thus he adheres to his agreement with God while the girl escapes the career for which he had promised her. The story is interesting mainly because it reveals the lingering of the old Covenant theology, which postulated a contractual relationship between God and human beings.

Parson Lord, in comparison with her earlier fiction, marks a distressing deterioration from which Freeman was only sporadically to rise. Not only have her subject matter and her treatment of it in that volume become trivial, but her prose style has totally lost its clipped, impressionistic quality. Conventionally long and complex sentences have replaced the short and simple structures of most of her earlier volumes. The diction is less concrete and more Latinized.

Satire and Humor

From the decade before Freeman's marriage in 1902 three volumes remain to be discussed. One, *Understudies,* can be better dealt with in the next chapter. The other two, humorous in nature, may be glanced at here. From 1895 to 1898 Freeman had written a series of sketches of stock village characters for the *Ladies' Home Journal.* In 1898 these were collected and published in a book entitled *People of Our Neighborhood.* It is difficult to understand why Van Wyck Brooks in *New Eng-*

land: Indian Summer ranked this little volume among Freeman's three or four best.[4] Though the book is pleasant reading, the characterization is all on the surface—a presentation of types rather than of individuals. Among the characters are "Timothy Sampson: The Wise Man," on whom the townspeople depend for every kind of service from doctoring their sick babies after the physician has failed to cure them to forecasting the weather on a day proposed for a picnic; "Cyrus Emett: The Unlucky Man," whose barns burn down as fast as he can rebuild them; "Nehemiah Stockwell," whose apple trees and potato fields yield produce when everybody else's fail and whose coddling by Providence arouses jealousy; "Phoebe Ann Little, the Neat Woman," who arises in cold horror in the middle of the night to make sure she has swept the cellar steps, for if they were dirty and she should die before morning her neighbors might remember her as untidy.

These and others are presented with great good humor but with no attempt to get to the roots of their salient traits. The approach is that of light comedy, in contrast to that of the more seriously analytic stories of the earlier collections. Written toward the end of the author's residence in Randolph, these sketches were modeled on her own neighbors, who tartly inquired whether Freeman thought she was so much better than they since she presumed to write about them in this manner.

In the same light vein and also written for the *Ladies' Home Journal* is the short novel *The Jamesons* (1899), which also received the praise of Van Wyck Brooks. It is one of Freeman's few attempts to exploit the conflicts in a country town between "natives" and summer people. Mrs. Jameson, who comes as a boarder to Linnville, sets about improving the village in general. She reads Browning at the Sewing Circle and recommends Ibsen and Maeterlinck for the Literary Club. A health faddist, she attempts to supplant the local diet of pies and poundcake with edibles that are hygienic but tasteless. At first resentful, the populace becomes merely amused when, having purchased a farm, Mrs. Jameson makes her chickens wear booties so that they won't scratch up the garden, mentions that she is "digging" squash and "picking" potatoes, and refuses to buy a cow whose upper teeth are missing. Her love of antiques amazes the townspeople, as does her use of bean pots for vases. When her daughter, after much opposition on both sides, marries the son of a prominent village family, harmony between Mrs. Jameson and the community is finally established.

Last Years at Randolph

In 1897, the same year in which she published *Jerome,* Freeman had become engaged to marry Dr. Freeman. A year or so later the engagement was temporarily broken, partly because Freeman thought that she was needed in the Wales family, with whom she lived in Randolph. During this period her sleep was disturbed by nightmares, and she had to resort to sedatives in such quantities that she became partly addicted to them. She needed now to sleep near someone who would hear her during her dreams and arouse her from them. In her waking reveries she seems sometimes to have pictured herself as a renegade from God's ordering of things—a rebel and an outcast.

The evidence of this state of mind is in a fragment of manuscript written much later and published for the first time in Edward Foster's biography of Freeman,[5] apparently part of a story that she never completed. In it an unmarried woman, Jane Lennox, living in her family homestead in a small town, agonizes over the state of her soul. Her life is solitary and uneventful; yet she is convinced that she is a powerful and rebellious force pitted against "the Whole," and she is certain that in small ways she has done unquestionable harm. She gloats over minor wrongs done her by her neighbors, for they make her feel superior. Though she has attempted to rise above her meannesses, she has been unsuccessful, for she cannot change her basic self. Actually Jane Lennox seems rather pleased with her shortcomings, as does Dostoyevski's underground man over his. She speculates that she might have been different if she had not been denied marriage and children—her "birthright," as she calls it, echoing the final paragraph of "A New England Nun." She concludes that she is far from a normal woman, married or not. She believes that she is a "monster" and takes pleasure in being so, as well as in her ability, which she shares with the Devil, to break God's laws.

One should be wary of judging an author by the characters in his or her stories. Yet this Lennox fragment is so unlike everything that Freeman ever published—for example, she seldom wrote in the first person, as she did in this (an exception is *The Heart's Highway*)—that critics have understandably wondered how closely it reflects Freeman's state of mind during her last years in Randolph. Foster attributes the mood betrayed in the story as stemming from Freeman's highly developed New England conscience, lacerating herself and rebelling "against the terms of freedom itself," describing her "neurotic pride with extraordinary precision," and "looking hard at herself, much harder than is customary among most troubled women."[6] On the other hand, Leah Blatt Glasser believes that this fragment is a statement, presumably Freeman's own, of the "rage, fear, disillusionment . . . in the life of a single woman";[7] and Michele Clark finds in it an expression of a woman's shame and anger at being a spinster.[8] A more fascinating comment is that of Ann Douglas Wood, who sees the elements of witchcraft in Jane Lennox's mental state.[9] Wood points out that to Freeman, as evidenced in *Giles Corey,* people become witches because of "repression and frustration."[10] But, Wood argues, Freeman's own life was plagued by repression and frustration. Also, she was plagued by shyness, reclusiveness (she once asserted that she did not like people), and the various neurotic symptoms already mentioned. In addition, of course, witches have the power to blight lives; and, Wood continues, "Freeman, who had lost a lover, a sister, a mother and a father in a short space of time in her young womanhood, must surely have felt this power was hers."[11] One cannot share the full implications of Wood's hypothesis. Clearly Freeman did not consider herself a witch; nor, of course, did Wood consider her actually to be one. Yet as a fictional character Jane Lennox may qualify as a witch and was intentionally presented as such by Freeman, who had written a play on Salem witchcraft. It is not unreasonable to assume that Jane Lennox is a product of Freeman's own tormented state of mind at various times of her life, but beyond this assumption we cannot go.

Chapter Nine
Literary Vaudeville
A Change of Scene

On New Year's Day, 1902, after many postponements during the preceding two years, Mary Wilkins and Dr. Charles Freeman were quietly married in Metuchen, New Jersey. The marriage turned out to be a very unhappy one, though in the early years things went smoothly enough.

Freeman was already acquainted with Metchuen, having often visited there as a guest of the *Harper's* editor, Henry Alden, and his wife. Within easy commuting distance of New York City, Metuchen was considered one of the most attractive of the city's suburbs, and because of the intellectual brilliance of some of its residents had become known as "The Brainy Borough." It had been settled in the seventeenth century by New Englanders as part of the township of Woodridge. When Freeman came there to live its population was about fifteen hundred. The change of scene from Randolph to Metuchen could not have been too traumatic.[1]

As the wife of a leading citizen and a friend of the Aldens, as well as a widely known author, Freeman was, of course, cordially received socially. She made many friends, got along well with her husband's mother and sisters, took pleasure in her role as a housekeeper, and was enthusiastic about the new house soon to be built from the proceeds of her writing. The crucial question was how the change would affect her as a literary artist. On this score Freeman herself was initially optimistic, assuring an interviewer from the *New York Herald* that she was going to write "a story about New Jersey life. Do you know that New Jersey is full of romance, as full as it is of mosquitoes? Yes, indeed, if I'd been born and brought up in Metuchen I'd have found just as quaint and romantic people to write about here in New Jersey as ever stepped though the pages of a New England story book. For people are all alike, especially if they happen to be women, whether they live in Massachusetts or Metuchen."[2] Yet as time passed she lost her enthusiasm. In a letter written to Carolyn Wells, who lived in nearby Rahway, she complained: "I have not a blessed thing to write about. . . . I read a crazy diary in a paper last night which just about fits a Metuchenite. It was something like this. Jan. 8. shook my head 17 times. Jan. 9. shook my head twenty times. Jan. 19. shook my head eight times."[3]

Dr. Freeman was eager to have his wife continue her writing, apparently viewing it as a lucrative source of income. He resented, in fact, her hours spent in cooking or other household chores because they cut into time and energy that he thought could be more profitably used in authorship. Always prolific, however, she did not slacken her writing pace. According to one report, she simultaneously used two typewriters, "on each of which was a novel." She would sit down to write not knowing what would come, allowing thought to suggest thought. In this manner she could turn out seven thousand words a day. Though she wrote without planning, relying entirely on "inspiration," she revised three or four times.[4] As always, the variety of her output was astonishing: animal stories, ghost stories, a novel written in competition with a British author, a "cooperative novel," melodrama, not to mention a steady flow of standard fiction of all lengths. For sheer versatility she had become a skilled literary vaudevillist,[5] which is not necessarily to denigrate her.

Yet, with a number of exceptions, Freeman's writing after her marriage declined in quality. One reason, of course, was the frantic pace at which she wrote. Though she had always written copiously and had frequently complained of overwork, there now were new demands on her time. Furthermore, her husband was not a restful man to live with. Always a frequenter of taverns, his drinking finally became so excessive as to necessitate sojourns in a sanatorium. After World War I his mind became affected by alcoholism, and his wife had to commit him to the New Jersey State Hospital for the Insane. Escaping in 1921, he returned home, apparently much improved. But soon he began drinking Prohibition liquor, and he had to be sent back to the asylum. Released once more, he lived for a time at home but later moved into his chauffeur's house. His wife obtained a legal separation, and Dr. Freeman drew up a will in favor of the chauffeur. When he died in 1923, the widow, who had been cut off with a dollar, and Dr. Freeman's four sisters, who had been left only two hundred dollars each, successfully contested the will. But by this time Freeman, now in her seventies, had virtually ceased to write. She had kept up top productivity, in fact, for only about a decade after her marriage.

The best of the fiction that she wrote during the Metuchen years continued to have New England settings and themes. In three novels, however, she did draw on her new environment during this period: *The Debtor* (1905), in which the main character was suggested by a former resident of Metuchen; *"Doc" Gordon* (1906), which is laid in a rural New Jersey town; and *The Butterfly House* (1912), a satire on the doings of a women's club modeled on the Metuchen Quiet Hour Club, which had admitted Freeman as a member shortly after her marriage. It is notable that these three novels are among the poorest of Freeman's writings. A fourth novel, *By the Light of the Soul* (1906), laid partly in New Jersey and partly in New England, is of somewhat better quality.

A Venture into the Supernatural

As early as 1903 the deterioration in Freeman's art became painfully noticeable in a volume with the title *The Wind in the Rose-Bush and Other Tales of the Supernatural*. Deficient in suspense and atmosphere, these stories rely on generally ludicrous devices for their interest: persistently appearing shadows on a wall; items of a dead woman's wardrobe that shuttle in and out of a closet in the chamber in which she died; spectral laundry hanging in a vacant lot near a haunted house; a rose blossom that detaches itself from a bush and comes to rest on a dead girl's bed. Indeed, in some cases Freeman seems to be striving for humor, though not very successfully.

It has been suggested that Freeman "attributes her ghosts to the evil potential of the individual will," as did Henry James in his stories of the supernatural.[6] This is true of at least one of Freeman's stories, "The Southwest Chamber," in which she employs Hawthorne's device of using a mirror to reveal latent evil in her protagonist. Yet with the exception of an occasional flash of the author's old flair for presenting village characters, these stories are undistinguished. She did much better in three ventures into the supernatural in her earlier fiction. One of these, "A Symphony in Lavender," in *A Humble Romance*, has been discussed in chapter 3. Two other stories, "A Faraway Melody" in *A Humble Romance* and "A Gentle Ghost" in *A New England Nun,* explore the supernatural. The first, in which the deaths of two sisters are each preceded by strains of distant music audible only to the one about to die, is remarkable for its recording of the placid monotony of the sisters' lives and its evocation of the springtime peace of a country village.

In the second story, "A Gentle Ghost," the realistic settings of a poor-house and a cemetery as viewed by a group of gossiping women do much to neutralize the excessively sentimental plot, which focuses on a little girl who finds a ghostly playmate among the graves.

Six Trees

Yet, in the same year as *The Wind in the Rose-Bush,* appeared a volume containing some writing equal to Freeman's best—a collection of short stories entitled *Six Trees,* which reflects vividly the tendency toward mysticism that had been increasingly apparent in her work ever since *Pembroke.*

"Who shall determine," Freeman asks, "the limit at which the intimate connection and reciprocal influence of all forms of visible life upon one another may stop? A man may cut down a tree and plant one. Who knows what effect the tree may have upon the man, to his raising or undoing?"[7] The answer to these questions is embodied in *Six Trees* and in another earlier collection, *Understudies* (1901). Between human beings and the living environment are "parallels, separated perhaps by the width of the eternity of the spirit, yet as perfect and undeviating as any on the terrestrial globe."[8] The answer, of course, is completely in accord with the views of Emerson, who saw all nature as a metaphor of spirit. What one sees, hears, touches, and smells are projections of what one thinks, intuits, or surmises. The world of the spirit and that of the senses are two sides of the same coin. Nowhere has this Emersonian doctrine, which is the touchstone of transcendentalism, been incorporated into fiction so consciously and so successfully as in these two books.

Six Trees, especially, has won the admiration of critics; and Freeman herself liked these stories the best of all her work.[9] In them she not only has full control of her craft but she has given fullest expression to the nature mysticism that seemed to be becoming a religion with her. In no way was this trend irreconcilable with the modified orthodoxy of her childhood. Indeed, the concept of nature as a divine metaphor or allegory was commonplace among the Puritans. One finds it basic, also, in Emily Dickinson's writings as well as in Emerson's, and it is important in Jonathan Edwards's autobiography.

A scanner of bibliographies might pass over *Six Trees* as a collection of stories held together by the gimmick of assigning to each an arboreal name. And *Understudies* might be dismissed as a double gimmick—

one group of stories in it named after animals and a second after flowers. But these tales and sketches are more than literary legerdemain. Animals, flowers, and trees are as central to them as to Ovid's *Metamorphoses*. In fact, consciously or unconsciously Freeman was carrying on the Ovidian tradition. She was writing of transformations just as the Roman poet did; only hers are spiritual rather than physical. Thus in "The Lombardy Poplar," in *Six Trees,* the tall slender tree, after which the story is named, typifies to an elderly single woman the self-sufficiency that she needs to break out of a lifelong subserviency to the opinion of others. Contrary to her cousin's view, she thinks the tree is beautiful; and when taken to task for expressing herself so independently, she retorts: "I'm sick of things and folks that are just like everything and everybody else. I'm sick of trees that are just trees. I like one that ain't" (148–49). The ensuing quarrel is no doubt petty and foolish, but marks the emergence of the spinster into something like selfhood. Previously she had been dominated by a now dead twin sister, whose overbearing place in her life has been taken by the cousin. Her recognition of the individuality of the tree is the first step toward a recognition of her own. Her life has been transformed into something shapely and complete like the poplar.

Similarly, in "The Elm-Tree" an old man's bitterness is transformed into tranquil acceptance when he climbs the boughs of a great elm and, harmlessly insane, finds there the shelter that a child finds in the arms of its mother. Though he has lost his reason, he is nevertheless at peace—a change not to be scorned. In "The White Birch," however, an equally unfortunate old man is brought by contemplation of a birch tree to a perfectly sane realization of "the dearness of that which is always left in the treasure-house of nature for those who are robbed" (64) of life's more sought-after goods.

Other transformations from discontent to peace of mind are recorded in "The Apple-Tree" and in "The Balsam Fir." The former presents an interesting contrast between two households—one slovenly but happy, the other spotlessly neat and conventional but unhappy. The village which is the scene of the story is described in idyllic terms: "There was no wealth in the village, there was even poverty, but everywhere thrift and making the most of little, bringing out of humble possessions the very utmost that was in them of beauty and utility. When a house was scarcely larger than a child's toy it was white-painted and green-blinded, with windows shining like jewels; when there was only a little patch of yard, it was gay with flowers or velvet-smooth with grass;

before it was a white fence or a trim green hedge, outside was a row of carefully tended trees" (171–72). Here was a New England village at its rare best, a place of thrift, respectability, neatness—and rigidity. But there is one discordant note, the Maddox family, who live in a decrepit house, its roof and sills sagging and its windowpanes broken, situated in a yard full of weeds, chickens, and scantily clad, barefooted urchins. But there is in the yard a gloriously blooming apple tree— "the one redemption" (173) of the surrounding squalor. In the doorway the husband lounges and admires the tree; the wife, inside in a rocking chair by a window, holds a wailing baby in her lap and reads a cheap novel. In short, the Maddoxes violate every time-honored local standard as to how people should live.

Across the street from the Maddox menage live an elderly couple, Sarah and Edison Blake, whose house is immaculate inside and out as a result of Sarah's obsessive cleanliness and orderliness. The stronger willed of the two, she tirelessly drives her husband into the service of her obsession. He is an overfat nobody; she is joyless, rigid, and overbearing, and she looks upon the Maddoxes with hostile contempt. The Blake household meets the village standards, in the letter if not in the spirit; the contrast with the Maddox household is that of opposites. Yet for the Blakes, clinging to their Puritan ethic of work and distrust of pleasure, life has gone sour. For the Maddoxes, despite their ramshackle dwelling, there is joy in their marriage and children. Also, there is beauty, as symbolized by the magnificent apple tree, which Sarah Blake looks at only grudgingly from across the street, asserting that she cares only for the fruit an apple tree produces and cares nothing for its blooms. The point of the story is clear, of course: beauty and joy have their source within the human soul, not in a code of behavior handed down from generation to generation. Freeman is championing the village pariahs, pointing out that custom-bound New England rigidity may be the death of joy.

Another possible dimension of the story has been suggested. Sarah is constantly shaking the dust out of her living-room mat, which may represent her own purity subdued by her husband's past sexual intrusions. At any rate, at the time of the story, sexuality in Sarah has been repressed to nonexistence. Across the street, however, the husband and wife have obviously given rein to their sexuality, living in what Sarah would call filth, yet enjoying living. The story is one of many in which Freeman, somewhat indirectly perhaps, comments on the effects of suppressed sexuality in the rural communities about which she writes.[10] It is worth noting, also, that with the Maddoxes uninhibited sexuality makes for harmony and respect between husband and wife. In their relationship there is no evidence of dominance of one over the other.

All the stories in *Six Trees* contain a delicate symbolism appropriate to the lives of the people involved. All are told with a sure descriptive skill and with convincing characterization. But most remarkable in the collection is "The Great Pine." A sailor, returning home after many years at sea, to the rocky hill-farm and the wife and child he had rebelliously deserted, gets lost in the wild terrain through which he is walking. Time and again he circles back to a certain lofty pine. Freeman describes the tree in terms of the songs the wind sings among its myriad branches—songs of winter in the summer and songs of summer in the winter—for always the voice evoked in its listeners thoughts "of that which was past and to come, rather than of the present" (69). After a number of circlings back to the tree, the sailor, still a rebel, sets fire to the forest in his anger—an act of spite against God. But as with so many of Freeman's rebellious characters, there is latent in the sailor a force that pulls him back into harmony with his lot. Following the usual sequence in Freeman's psychology, the act of rebellion stimulates this harmonizing tendency. The sailor turns back and extinguishes the fire before it destroys the tree. For the first time he has risen "superior to his own life. . . . He, through saving the tree from himself, gained a greater spiritual growth than the tree had gained in height since it first quickened with life" (79).

No longer walking in circles, the sailor takes his way directly home to the lonely farmhouse from which he had vanished years ago. He does not find his wife, or his wife's mother, for both have died. But living in the house he finds his wife's second husband—she thought her first one had drowned—who is half dead with consumption. There are also two children, one his own and the other the stranger's. The sailor still moves directly, not faltering in his course. With an unprecedented burst of energy he cuts wood to sell, buys a horse, paints the house, and stocks the cellar with food. He nurses the man who had supplanted him as his wife's husband and befriends the child of that union. Like so many of Freeman's characters in these and other stories, he has found his spiritual center. The act of saving the tree was the act of discovery. Later the tree blows down in a winter gale, but the man stands firm in spirit, transformed into something more durable than timber.

Understudies

Animals and flowers are the subjects of the earlier book of meta-morphoses, *Understudies.* The title is a clever one. Not only are the animals and flowers lower in the organic scale—that is, they are *under* the human species—but also in many of the stories they are approximate duplications of human beings, understudies in the theatrical sense. Thus the peony in the story named for it typifies the obese woman whose favorite flower it is. The arethusa, a flower of secluded marshlands, establishes itself in the soul of a young girl who annually visits it in its lonely habitat. She identifies the retiring, beautiful blossom with the inviolable center of her own heart. Even on the day of her wedding she visits the flower, for she hopes that there will always exist in her something untouchable even by a husband. In another story, "Bouncing Bet," the flower growing in the weed-choked yard of a dilapidated mansion represents the tenacity of an elderly spinster, the last offshoot of a once-proud family, who clings to her ancestral home despite the efforts of her relatives and the town's selectmen to uproot her.

The flowers are symbols in the profoundest sense. They are integral parts of people's lives, part of their grasp not only of reality but, more important, of their own identities. This relationship is true even more markedly of the animal understudies. In "The Monkey," a boy and the animal are united in their mischievous, almost destructive high spirits. There is a mutual accommodation of one to the other until, in spirit and behavior, each is transformed into the other. Similarly in "The Squirrel," a farmer's sympathy for the animal whose hoard of nuts he has accidentally discovered and confiscated eventuates in his replacing the stolen supply with a bushel of walnuts bought at the local store. The way of life of both farmer and squirrel is based on conserving the growth of the summer for use in the winter. In the resemblance of the means of survival the farmer senses a more profound resemblance that forces upon him, the more spiritually developed being, this act of restoration.

Most sensitive of the animal stories are "The Cat" and "The Doctor's Horse." The former, which deals with Freeman's favorite animal, opens with a description of the cat hunting a rabbit in a snowstorm high up on a mountainside. Having captured its prey, the cat returns to the lonely shack, deserted in winter, where in warmer months it lives with its recluse master. After the cat's return to the cabin, an intruder breaks in. The cat gives him the rabbit and the two share it. All winter the arrangement continues: the cat brings game which the man cooks and scrupulously shares with the animal. The barrier between two kingdoms is partly breached. They live in partnership almost as equals.

In "The Doctor's Horse" the relationship between man and beast is more complex. A strong-willed doctor breaks a recalcitrant horse. But one day the horse, left in the control of a timorous girl, runs away. Intractable from then on, the horse has to be sold. But years later, the doctor, his health shattered, unknowingly buys the same horse, which is now old and submits as formerly to the doctor's will. The doctor finally discovers that he is driving his former animal and with the discovery some of his youthful confidence is revived. In their last years, man and beast complement each other, each adding to the other's strength and contentment.

These animal, flower, and tree stories are germane to a consideration of Freeman as a symbolist in the tradition of Hawthorne. To begin with, they were not her first attempts in this line. In "A New England Nun" the caged canary is an unobtrusive representation of Louisa's own caged life, ruffled like the bird's feather's when threatened by masculine coarseness. "An Object of Love" deals with the relation, half affection and half resentment, of an elderly woman and her cat. Plants and animals are, of course, important in the quiet lives of villagers like those about whom Freeman writes. If one lives for long in close proximity to a tree or a horse, a relationship of some depth, complexity, and significance is likely to develop, especially in the absence of the distractions of modern life. Many precedents influenced Freeman in these stories. Hawthorne's use of chickens and plants in *The House of the Seven Gables* could not have been lost on her. Jewett's "A White Heron," the story of the influence of a noble pine tree and a rare and beautiful bird upon a child's spirit and character, was a favorite of Freeman's. Indeed, both she and Jewett go beyond Hawthorne—to whom both admitted a debt—in that their trees, birds, and animals are not only symbols or projections of character but also objects that interact with human personalities and are formative of character. American literature abounds in such relationships: Poe and his raven; the crew of the *Pequod* and the White Whale; the boy, the bear, and the dog in Faulkner's "The Bear"; the rancher and the black panther in Walter Van Tilburg Clark's *The Track of the Cat*; the woman and the flowers in Steinbeck's "Chrysanthemums"; and Santiago and the marlin in Hemingway's *The Old Man and the Sea*.

An Intercontinental Tournament

In 1907 the *New York Herald* conceived a circulation-building stunt without parallel in literary history—an Anglo-American novel-writing competition in which Freeman would represent the United States and Max Pemberton would represent England. Not only was this to be a contest between nations but a duel between two schools of fiction as well. Freeman was to write a "realistic novel of New England life," *The Shoulders of Atlas,* which would be pitted against Pemberton's "swashbuckling romance of Old England." Installments of each were to be printed weekly in the *Herald's* Sunday edition. Readers were invited to vote each week on their preference, using ballots printed in the newspaper. The winner in a final cumulative count would receive $5,000. In the full-page announcement of the contest in the magazine section of the *Herald* was an illustration of Freeman mounted on a prancing white American Pegasus facing John Bull astride a black charger. As it turned out, to write her book, which would number about a hundred thousand words, Freeman had only two months. She was doubtless spurred into this grueling assignment by the need to pay for a $20,000 house that she and her husband were planning. The prize, which she easily won, plus serial and book rights netted her exactly this sum. The novel was the most profitable of her literary ventures.[11]

An undisputed financial success by any standards, *The Shoulders of Atlas,* despite the pressure under which it was written and the ballyhoo accompanying its publication, possessed more literary merit than any other novel that Freeman wrote after her marriage. Its tone is genuinely realistic, if one overlooks the final chapter with its multiple weddings. The plot, though bordering on melodrama, is believable. The suspicion that a schoolteacher of doubtful moral character—who has died (either intentionally or accidentally) by overdosing on arsenic that she had been taking for her complexion—was actually murdered occurs only to the pettier and more neurotic townspeople. Neither the police nor the responsible citizens believe it. In addition, the contention of one critic that the plot hinges too much on "a hocus-pocus of concealed and altered wills"[12] is an exaggeration. Only one will has been concealed, and it has not been altered. It has no validity since it had not been signed, and it was superseded by another completely legal one.

The only conflict arising from the existence of the two wills is in the mind of the heroine, Sylvia Whitman. Though she has inherited a house and some property perfectly legally from a distant cousin, her discovery of an older will works upon her New England conscience until she is convinced that she is holding what rightly belongs to the young and pretty relative mentioned in the will, Rose Fletcher, now residing with her in the inherited house. The earlier will is a stimulus that prods Sylvia's conscience into more violent activity. Before she discovered it, she had been uneasy about the inheritance. Had she not discovered it, she would have found other grounds for self-accusation.

Sylvia Whitman, indeed, is one of Freeman's New Englanders of indomitable volition linked to a hypersensitive conscience. Eager to accept the legacy, which lifts her and her husband out of a lifetime of oppressive poverty, she is quick to find reasons to make herself miserable in spite of (in fact, because of) her good luck. For months her will is in mortal combat with her conscience. The deadlock is broken when, in accord with Puritan tradition, she makes public confession—at Rose's wedding. Though informed by a lawyer present that she holds the property legally, she persists in her self-flagellation: "I was just as guilty, . . . for I had the knowledge of sin in my heart and I held it there. I was just as guilty."[13] To this daughter of the Puritans the knowledge of sin was sweeter than that of innocence.

The Shoulders of Atlas does indeed dwell heavily upon the psychic abnormalities latent in a New England village. Sylvia's morbidly sensitive conscience is, of course, nothing new. But her attachment to Rose, though she herself regards it as maternal, is clearly homosexual. She is physically attracted to the girl, to the pinkness and softness of her flesh; insists on undressing her at bedtime, though Rose is a grown woman; restrains herself only with great exertion from embraces far from maternal, and fights with hysterical ferocity against the girl's marrying. The desire to keep Rose is as strong as her wish to keep the money she erroneously thinks is Rose's. Eliza Farrell, the schoolteacher supposedly poisoned by her landlady, is even more obviously homosexual. Though she is locally considered single, she has been married but was deserted by her husband shortly after the wedding. Now aging, she desperately struggles to retain her beauty with cosmetics. Though she seems anxious to attract men, she excites their repulsion rather than admiration: "She loved women better than a woman usually does, and women could not abide her" (78).

In East Westland, the village in which *The Shoulders of Atlas* is laid, neuroses of sexual origin are endemic. Hysteria is as rife as in seventeenth-century Salem, where sexual jealousies and frustrations—at least according to Freeman's *Giles Corey*—vied with religious fear and bigotry in producing abnormal behavior. In East Westland the death of the disturbing Eliza Farrell under slightly suspicious circumstances catches the imagination of the oversexed Lucy Ayres. She attempts to feed poison candy to Rose, who is her rival for the affections of Horace Allen, the young principal of the local high school. In a novel written after 1920 Lucy would have been depicted as a nymphomaniac, which she latently was. But her position in a respectable family in a strait-laced New England town completely frustrates her supercharged libido and drives her into pathological conduct. Freeman comments: "She was a thing always devoured but never consumed by a flame of nature, because of a lack of food to satisfy an inborn hunger" (175). She throws herself at Horace, much to his embarrassment; but he has the intelligence to understand "the helplessness of the young things before forces of nature of which they were brought up in so much ignorance" (179). Thus Freeman has taken into account as in none of her earlier works the force of sexuality in shaping the lives of her characters.

The causation that Freeman ascribes to the hysteria of Lucy and to some extent to the abnormality of Eliza Farrell is essentially deterministic—a point of view that was becoming increasingly noticeable in her writing after 1900. The thesis of *The Shoulders of Atlas* is that every human being groans under an almost unbearable burden that Atlas himself could support only with the greatest difficulty. Some of these burdens, like Sylvia's sense of guilt, the sufferer may have a fair chance of removing or at least lightening by his or her own efforts. But others, like Eliza's and Lucy's sexual compulsions, are beyond the individual's control. One learns to bear them or succumbs, as does Lucy, who becomes temporarily insane. Such a burden, as Lucy's mother says, "may bend innocence into guilt and modesty into shamelessness, but there is no more reason for condemnation than in a case of typhoid fever" (178).

The Shoulders of Atlas received much acclaim at the time of its publication. Purporting to be a realistic book, it explored facets and depths of village life not hitherto alluded to in American fiction. In her probings of the libido—though Freeman at that time would hardly have known the Freudian term—she uncovered elements in the human will that even she may not have understood. Yet, especially as the wife of a physician, she must have long been aware of the phenomena she was dissecting.

A curious aspect of *The Shoulders of Atlas* is a critical attitude toward women that is not evident in Freeman's earlier writing. Frequently she puts into the mouths of her male characters disparaging remarks about women as compared to men. Many of these reflect popularly held stereotypes and perhaps should not be taken as indicative of the novelist's views. But more significant, as well as surprising, are some of the authorial comments. Of Sylvia Whitman as she confronts her husband Henry, Freeman writes: "She was New England austerity and conservatism embodied. She was terrifying, although it would have puzzled anybody to have told why. Certain it was that no man would have had the temerity to contest her authority as she stood there" (219–20). The word "terrifying," which Freeman would not have considered complimentary, reveals a changed attitude toward strong-willed New England women, with whom, in previous works, she was usually sympathetic. This is true even of Deborah Thayer in *Pembroke,* who is Sylvia's equal in "austerity and conservatism" but is not described as "terrifying." Again, in reporting Henry's musings, Freeman writes: "He was thinking how women were reeds driven by the winds of their emotions, and really, in a measure, irresponsible" (251)—a judgment that seems as much Freeman's as Henry's. And, indeed, throughout the book Sylvia seems out of control of her emotions and prone to unreasonable assumptions and actions.

Freeman's characterizations of the other three important women in the novel are equally critical. Rose Fletcher is little more than a simpering doll—a woman in the worst tradition of the empty-headed heroine of sentimental fiction. Her permitting herself to be mauled by Sylvia and her temporary bowing to Sylvia's objections to her marriage indicate absence of will and judgment. One can only assume that Freeman considered her a rather sorry specimen of womanhood. Eliza Farrell and Lucy Ayres with their sexual compulsions are, to repeat, unlike any women previously to appear in Freeman's writings. She attempts to treat their problems understandingly. Yet she endows Lucy with what amounts to the evil eye as, rearing "her pretty back with a curious, snake-like motion" (140), she glares at Rose, her rival for Horace's love. As Ann Douglas Wood observes, Lucy seems to possess some of the characteristics and powers of a witch.[14] Similarly, Eliza Farrell, rejected as she has been by her husband and others, detects in herself something evil and ophidian, telling Horace, "I might as well be a snake as a woman"; and despite her elaborate efforts, suggestive of magic, to preserve her beauty, she felt that "she excited repulsion rather than affection in everybody with whom she came in contact." And Horace believes that there is truth in all this, though he does not know why (77). Both these women bring to mind Jane Lennox and her strange "power" in the unpublished fragment discussed earlier, for she too was reacting to rejection.

Compared to these women in *The Shoulders of Atlas* the men are distressingly commonplace. Horace is a personable, somewhat intelligent man, well-liked by the women in the novel and, predictably, in love with Rose's pretty looks. Henry is a good man, a good enough husband; but, more interestingly, he is unable to adjust to his life of leisure made possible by his wife's inheritance. An operative since boyhood in a local shoe factory and always on the verge of poverty, he has bitterly resented being exploited for the enrichment of the manufacturers. But now he finds that he cannot live without the routine of drudgery that had been his lifelong lot; he returns to the factory and takes up his old work. As always with the poor, Freeman treats Henry with sympathy, but she does not gloss over his dullness. Finally, Sydney Meeks, a mildly eccentric bachelor who, as a lawyer, tries to guide the other characters through the complications of their lives, emerges as level-headed but rather uninteresting.

Throughout the novel there are comments on marriage, some of them authorial, others spoken by the characters. Lucy's mother, for example, points out to her daughter that "there are other things in life [than marriage], or it would be monstrous" (154). Sylvia, of course, has her own reasons for wishing to keep Rose unmarried and living with her, but there may be more than a selfish motive in many of her remarks; for example, "Rose has got enough to live on, and what any girl that's got enough to live on wants to get married for beats me" (191), for "marriage is an awful risk" (204). Lawyer Meeks, who has had disappointments in love, is pictured as happy in his celibate state, as are many other people, mainly women, in Freeman's works. When she wrote *The Shoulders of Atlas,* Freeman herself was in her middle fifties and by all accounts her marriage, after five years, had not yet soured. Yet in this novel, though at its end she conventionally arranges weddings for all the single persons available, she examines as never before the institution of matrimony and seriously speculates as to whether it is the sole avenue to a woman's happiness—as indeed she must have wondered most of her life.

"Doc" Gordon

As a promotional device the international contest was crude, though Freeman's efforts resulted in a work of some literary merit. A year

before the contest *"Doc" Gordon* (1906), which Freeman herself called
a "frightful" and "bad" novel, had been published in an equally bizarre
manner.[15] The publishers—the Authors and Newspapers Association
of New York—released to only one bookshop in any city the right to
sell the book, and the name of the shop was printed in the copies that
it sold. Freeman's estimate of the novel is accurate: it is an unabashed
attempt at melodrama with an utterly preposterous plot. The "Doc"
himself—a hard drinker and a practical joker, as was Dr. Freeman—is
a somewhat interesting character, as are several village eccentrics. The
plot revolves around two moral dilemmas that the "Doc" faces: whether
he was justified in causing the death of a man who threatens to murder
him; and whether he was right in terminating by euthanasia the terrible sufferings of his wife during the last hours of a fatal illness. It is
interesting that Freeman should raise these problems. The presentation
of the would-be murderer as an amoral being, no more responsible for
his actions than is a venomous snake for using its fangs, is a foretaste
of the deterministic thinking that reappeared a year later in *The Shoulders of Atlas.* More startling, but in line with the growing skepticism
of the times, was her recognition, as the "Doc" puts it, of "injustice
on the part of the Higher Power."[16] But this drift from Christian orthodoxy was not for long. To the end of her life Freeman clung to the
humanized Calvinism of her girlhood.

A Cooperative Novel

What with the Anglo-American contest and the experiment with
melodrama, this was a time of literary showmanship for Freeman. The
trend continued with her part in a cooperative novel titled *The Whole
Family* (1908), consisting of twelve chapters, each one assigned to a
prominent author of the day. The first eleven chapters were supposedly
contributions of various members of a family; the twelfth was by an
outsider. The idea was William Dean Howells's; the editorial responsibility was that of Elizabeth Jordan, editor of *Harper's Bazar,* in which
it was to be published serially. Among the twelve contributors were
Howells himself, Alice Brown, Henry James, and Elizabeth Stuart
Phelps (Ward). Howells, representing the father of the family, wrote
an actionless first chapter of what was clearly to be a love story. Freeman, in the role of "The Old-Maid Aunt," wrote the second chapter,
depicting the aunt not as the stereotyped spinster that Howells had
envisaged in his chapter—that is, a submissive woman who, unmarried

at thirty, put on a cap and, in Freeman's phrase, "renounced the world"[17]—but as a woman who has remained single by choice, dresses stylishly, and is attractive to men younger than she. Howells, she asserted, was hopelessly behind the times. Thus her "old-maid aunt" finds that the fiancé of her niece (only fourteen years younger than she) is in love with her—an embarrassing situation, since the young couple's wedding is about to take place. Freeman's motives were complex. She was displeased with Howells's stereotyping of the aunt in chapter 1; after all, Freeman at the age of forty-nine had married a man seven years her junior. Also, she hoped to "start some action or plot, or rather indicate a plot."[18] Howells was outraged and begged Elizabeth Jordan to reject Freeman's chapter; but Jordan, herself unmarried at forty, liked the chapter and printed it.

Jordan likened the whole project to a production by P. T. Barnum, but somehow she controlled her twelve prima donnas and brought the novel to completion, bluntly describing it as "a mess."[19] Yet it was at least a curiosity if of slight literary merit. Freeman's chapter, in fact, is well written; and, in the character of the aunt, she refreshingly rejected what she called the "hackneyed"[20] views of persons like Howells regarding spinsters and demonstrated that a woman may deliberately choose not to be married and do so without loss of dignity or attractiveness and lead a fully rewarding life.

Chapter Ten

The End of a Career and Final Reputation

The fiction discussed in the previous chapter represents Freeman's efforts to find fresh subjects and genres and to broaden her readership, and several of these efforts produced work of respectable quality. Along with this experimentation, she kept up a constant output of stories and novels of a more conventional or commonplace sort. In these writings the decline in her talent that marked her New Jersey years is apparent. Her move from Randolph to suburban Metuchen put her at a disadvantage. Her best writing had always been about New England country and village people. In her new environment she was removed from the materials and settings that she could handle most effectively; and though she still wrote about them some of the time, she was unable to put them to really effective use.

The Debtor

The two longest novels of this period, *The Debtor* (1905) and *By the Light of the Soul* (1906), have their settings wholly or in part in a New York City suburb like Metuchen. *The Debtor,* laid entirely in New Jersey, is essentially a silly story. Some of the intentional humor, to be sure, comes off reasonably well. One can smile at the wiles of the four-flusher Carroll, not an uncommon suburban type, as he dupes the tradespeople of Banbridge. These townsfolks are, of course, the "natives," residents from long before the commuters moved in; and as such, Freeman, the specialist in village character, makes them come to life. Most likable is Anderson, who is a lawyer turned grocer, a bachelor approaching middle age, who marries Carroll's daughter Charlotte. Charlotte herself, however, is enough to spoil the whole book. A simpering nincompoop, she is the product of a degree of sentimentality that Freeman had hitherto not displayed. More realistically conceived is Carroll's hatred for the business rival who has ruined him—a hatred so consuming that it becomes directed against himself and, in accord with the Freudian theory of suicide, almost leads him to take his own life. But an occasional psychological insight and several amusing characters are not enough to salvage over five hundred pages of fiction blemished by pervasive mawkishness and a preposterous plot. By any standards *The Debtor* is a failure. By the standards of Freeman's best work it is a disaster.

By the Light of the Soul

More can be said for *By the Light of the Soul,* an undertaking of some two hundred thousand words. The title indicates the novel's theme— the Emersonian notion that the soul itself is a source of insight adequate to guide us through the moral labyrinths of life. Friends of Freeman considered the book to be a spiritual autobiography. The heroine, Maria Edgham, in her childhood appears to be a replica of the child Mary Wilkins—a pretty, bright, somewhat spoiled, intensely sensitive girl. The religious growth of Maria, who was born into a New Jersey commuting family but was of New England stock on her mother's side, suggests her creator's tendency to combine a fairly orthodox Calvinism with a rather amorphous but apparently satisfying mysticism.

Learning as a young girl of her father's mortal illness, Maria mildly rebels against the God who serves so treacherously those who have kept their covenant with him. Without ceasing to attend church, she has certain reservations concerning the God of her fathers. But after her father's death, her religious sensitivity deepens, and she feels assured that her father had "gone to" God, and she now had intimations of Christ's "unutterable and eternal love. . . . It seemed to her for the first time she laid hold on life in the midst of death. She had a premonition that this state, which bordered on ecstasy, would not endure."[1] But if it does not endure, it returns with great intensity. At other times of deep emotional crisis, she has mystical insights that serve to confirm the rightness of her most difficult decisions; for example, on one occasion

she gazed up at the northern constellation, at the mysterious polar star, and it seemed to steady her mind and give it power to deal with her petty problem of life by its far-away and everlasting guiding light. . . . "There is the great polar star," she said to herself, "there are all the suns and stars, here is the earth, and here am I, Maria Edgham, who am on the earth, but must some day give up my mortal life, and become a part of it, and part of the material universe and perhaps also of the spiritual. I am as nothing, and yet this pain in my heart, this love in my heart, makes me shine with my own fire as much as the star. I could not be unless the earth existed, but it is of such as myself that the earth is made up, and without such as myself it could not shine in its place in the heavens. . . ." Then all at once, in a perfect flood of rapture, something which she had never before known came into her heart: the consciousness of the love of God for herself, of the need of God for herself. . . . The knowledge of the love of God was over her. She gazed up again at the great polar star . . . , and for the first time in her whole life the primitive instinct of worship asserted itself within her. (437–39)

Experiences such as Maria's are recorded elsewhere in Freeman's writings, for example, in "The Balking of Christopher" and also in *Pembroke* when on two occasions Barnabas experiences moments of something like rapture induced, in part, by the beauties of nature. Other instances may be found in *Six Trees* and in *Understudies*. It is evident that experiences like these occurred in Freeman's own life; and in her lengthy description of Maria Edgham's transport there is an unmistakable subjective ring.

Some readers have termed Maria Edgham a bore. Truly her customary dreary, unwavering seriousness, her will that can ruthlessly smother her most turbulent emotions if these in any way threaten to lead her from the straitest path of duty, her morbidly acute conscience, her fiercely determined charitableness toward the poor, and above all her readiness to condemn all others who fall short of her own superhuman standards—all these traits are tiresome. As Freeman frequently states, Maria comes from a long line of women of indomitable will. In her assurance of the rightness of her own views and acts Maria doubtless resembles an old-time Puritan convinced of membership in the community of saints. Yet in her moments of mystical insight as well as in her loyalty to her family, Maria ceases to be obnoxious. Certainly Freeman did not mean her to be obnoxious at all.

One reason that Maria, at times, becomes a bit ludicrous to the reader is that the plot of the novel provides only the feeblest motivation for her powers of will and endurance. The central device is a marriage, never consummated, that a dull-witted parson forced on her and a high-school classmate while the two were wandering in New York City in search of Maria's little sister, who had run away from home. Such a marriage, even if legal—which is doubtful, since no license had been secured—could have been annulled without the slightest difficulty and

with dishonor to no one. Yet the couple, who understandably hate each
other and seldom thereafter even nod to each other on the street, carry
their secret with them far into adulthood, abandoning any thought of
real marriage with other partners. Inevitably, of course, Maria's
younger sister Evelyn falls in love with Maria's "husband"; and equally
inevitably this occurs at the moment, deferred for fifteen years, when
Maria and her spouse are beginning to be attracted to each other and
are on the verge of entering into an actual union. Maria's willpower
and sense of duty surge. She flees, changes her name, and gets a report
printed that she is dead. The sister is free to marry her "brother-in-
law," and she does so. In the context of such tomfoolery, Maria's otherwise impressive and valid, if repelling, strength of character becomes
unconvincing and irrelevant.

Yet even this novel is not without some strength. It catches the
atmosphere of the New Jersey commuting town in which the first half
of the book is laid. Shifting to a Massachusetts mill city, as if Freeman
were seeking more familiar ground, the action becomes more credible;
and the setting continues to be interesting, especially the glimpses of
decay and demoralization in which people on the undesirable side of
the river live. Prostitution, drunkenness, and criminal neglect of children are presented with a "naturalism" that Crane or Dreiser would
find to their taste.

In *By the Light of the Soul,* Freeman voices more outspokenly than
ever before her awareness of human folly. As in many of her works,
there is a character who takes petty reprisals against destiny for assigning him to an unpleasant life, in this case life in an industrial town:
"He, Henry Stillman, actually had a conviction that he was showing
recrimination and wounding fate, which had so injured him, if only
with a pinprick, by staying away from church" (235). In earlier stories,
characters who rebel against fate—for example, the woman in "A Tardy
Thanksgiving"—retain some dignity; but Henry, as he thumbs his
nose at God by reading scandal sheets during church hours, merely
makes himself ridiculous.

Afterglow

Freeman had always done her most brilliant writing in short fiction.
During the New Jersey years she continued to pound through her type-
writer a steady flow of stories. Of these an occasional one ranked with
the best she had written, but the days of whole volumes of distin-

guished tales were past. Only a brief glance at these later collections is worthwhile.

The Givers (1904) is composed largely of Christmas stories. They are competent in their evocation of New England settings, especially of the blizzards and gales of December, and in their characterization. But they are sentimental in plot, as is usual for their genre. Yet few even of these are downright mawkish. The men and women solitaries who people them do, of course, have joy brought to their dreary existences in accord with the season—but the joy is always a lasting one, involving basic transformations of their lives. For example, two feuding spinster sisters get together after years of estrangement; a lonely hill-farmer finally marries the girl who had jilted him decades before; and like true New Englanders these people take their good fortune without undue display of emotion. Studies in generosity, the stories are at worst harmless and at best heart-warming.

In 1907 appeared *The Fair Lavinia and Others,* a volume of tales with titles like "Amarina's Roses," "Eglantina," and "The Willow-Ware," and dealing for the most part with small-town gentlefolk. Though originally printed in *Harper's New Monthly,* these tales are pretty much without substance. The only exception is "The Gold," laid in Revolutionary days and telling the story of a farmer who has a goldsmith convert his inherited precious metal into andirons, doorknobs, drawer handles, and the like, which he puts to their normal use about his house just as if they were made of brass. Having murdered the goldsmith, who alone knows what has been done with the gold, the farmer goes off to the army, refusing to tell his wife how the treasure is hidden. The wife ransacks the house and digs up every square foot of the farm. Eventually she is murdered by marauders seeking the supposed hoard. The farmer at last returns and lives out his life in poverty surrounded by wealth he dare not, and will not, use. As a tale of greed that destroys a human soul, this story carries considerable impact.

The next collection, *The Winning Lady and Others* (1909), was considered by some to be the best that Freeman had ever published—an estimate that is unfounded. First, in all her later stores and novels Freeman's style was gaining fluency and complexity at the expense of the unadorned simplicity and directness that had contributed so much to the effectiveness of her earlier work. Glibness was supplanting feeling and was draped like a veil between the author and her material. Second, her subject matter was becoming increasingly trivial and uninteresting. Both these tendencies are glaringly present in *The Winning*

Lady, and especially so in the title story recounting the doings of bridge-playing "ladies."

But at least three of the stories in the collection have true merit. Two of these—"Little-Girl-Afraid-of-a Dog" and "The Joy of Youth"— are effective in the manner in which they enter a child's mind; and, though they are written for adults, they explain Freeman's success in writing for children. In the first, ten-year-old Emmeline Ames is afflicted with a secret fear of a mongrel owned by a penniless family to whom she must deliver a daily gift of eggs from her mother's and her aunt's farm. So intense is her fear of the yapping little cur that her health suffers from it and causes her to have nightmares. But she will not tell her mother of her terror. "She had too much self-control for her own good, young as she was."[2] She is also too obedient, too conscientious, to think of not making her deliveries. A mere child, there exist in her a burgeoning New England conscience and the fierce will that afflicts so many of Freeman's characters. Ironically the mother and aunt think that the child's health is benefited by her daily walk in delivering the eggs. But Emmeline one day has a chance to lock the dog in a corncrib in an isolated field, and she can now make her deliveries unmolested. However, conscience intervenes; realizing that the dog is starving, she goes to the corncrib and feeds him, thereby winning his deepest canine devotion and removing the cause of her fear. According to Freeman, the episode has taught the girl a profound lesson: that love and compassion will banish fear, which is love's worst enemy.

Freeman's grasp of child psychology in this story (and in "The Joy of Youth," in which Emmeline is again the central figure) is sound. Moreover, always an animal lover, her handling of the little nondescript mongrel is utterly true. Finally, her depiction of rural poverty is as stark and appalling as in "Siter Liddy." Freeman once wrote to her editor at *Harper's Bazar,* Mary Booth: "No body knows how some of these country women, with large families, and small purses do work. O they are the ones I would help, if I were rich."[3] But the woman, Mrs. Ticknor, to whom Emmeline carries eggs seems not to inspire these feelings: "An enormous slatternly woman, a mountain of inert flesh, appeared. . . . Behind Mrs. Ticknor the close room swarmed with children—children with gaping, grinning faces, some of them with impudent faces, but most of them placidly inert like their mother. The Ticknors represented the very doldrums of humanity" (53). The father, a drunkard, works only sporadically to avert actual starvation. When Emmeline was still terrified by the dog, this scene of squalor added to her terror.

Most impressive among the several creditable stories in *The Winning Lady* is "Old Woman Magoun," which tells how a proud country-woman lets her dead daughter's illegitimate fourteen-year-old daughter eat the berries of deadly nightshade and die rather than permit her to be taken by her father, the degenerate son of a once respected family. By him she is to be used as payment of a debt to his lecherous gambling partner. One critic writes: "That sexual plunder threatens the innocence of a young girl is an obscenity for which the only plausible and exquisite option is death."[4] As a study in rural degeneracy, the story is unsurpassed in Freeman's writing. Drunkenness is rampant among the male characters in the story, and they are presented as lazy and incompetent workers. When her grandchild says, "Men ain't very nice, be they?" Old Woman Magoun answers, "No, they ain't, take them altogether" (265).

Freeman's final three novels deserve little attention. *The Yates Pride* (1912), a tiny volume, recounts the antics that a well-born but impoverished spinster goes through to conceal from "folks" the fact that she has been reduced to taking in laundry. The story is told in the words of gossiping neighbors. *The Butterfly House* (1912), as has been mentioned, is a satire on the pettiness of life among clubwomen in a New Jersey suburb obviously modeled on Metuchen. The preposterous plot hinges on one woman pretending to be the author of another woman's best-selling novel. Finally, in 1917, appeared *The Alabaster Box,* which Freeman originally intended to be a drama, but which she converted into a novel in collaboration with Florence Morse Kingsley, a popular American novelist herself. The improbable plot traces the fortunes of a small-town banker who embezzles money entrusted to him and goes to jail for eighteen years, after which he returns to his old home to live with his saintly daughter. The villagers descend on his house and stone it, driving the old man into the woods to die of starvation and exposure. As an exposé of villagers' capacity for hate the novel puts one in mind of Mark Twain's "The Man That Corrupted Hadleyburg," but as a literary work it does no credit to either of its authors. However, the Vitagraph Company of America found in it material for a motion picture, which was filmed in the same year as the book was published.

The Copy-Cat and Other Stories (1914) contains the last fiction of merit that Freeman wrote. The first six stories are about children in an unnamed village, apparently suburban but with many rural characteristics. The children are real, "as chokeful of mischief as a pod of peas."[5] Several of them appear in more than one story, as do some of the adults. The series provides a view of village life as lived by youngsters, and this life, as Freeman depicts it, is much less fraught with the clash of wills and the eruption of passions than that of the adult villagers in her usual stories. Avoiding sentimentality, these tales underscore the wholesomeness of small-town childhood, but the children are for the most part of prosperous families in a prosperous community that sends its progeny to a private school. In earlier collections or novels Freeman presented the spectacle of childhood blighted by extreme poverty both of spirit and of things.

In addition to truly delightful stories of childhood, *The Copy-Cat* contains several other stories of a quality that marks a real, if brief, resurgence of Freeman's talents. Among these are two stories of revolt. "Dear Annie" tells of a young woman's rebellion against exploitation by her sister and her weak-willed father, the village minister. The other story of revolt, "The Balking of Christopher," is one of the loveliest things Freeman ever wrote. In it the revolt is not against another person or a family but against God and the duty orthodox religion enjoins. All his life Christopher had tried to do his duty, and Providence had always thrown obstacles in his way—fire, drought, flood, sickness, death. One spring morning Christopher decides he will not do his duty, which that day is to plough the South Field. Instead he goes to the minister to ask a question: "Why did I come into the world without any choice?" (275). Since the question is a knotty one, to say the least, the minister fails to give an answer that satisfies Christopher; but he does listen to Christopher's description of what he plans to do. He intends to leave the farm for a time to live in solitude in a sugaring shack far up on a mountainside and enjoy there the changing seasons as his farming duties have never permitted him to do. Nothing will swerve this unlettered Thoreau from his purpose, and he moves to his mountain retreat. The minister, fascinated by the venture, periodically visits him, bringing supplies of food. But after a few months, Christopher comes down from the mountain, saying, "I've got rested for all my life" (290). He is settled in his mind now, he tells the minister. He will never complain again, no matter what happens. He has found "that all the good things and all the bad things that come to a man who tries to do right are just to prove to him that he is on the right path. . . . I have found out the answer to my 'Why?' . . . I have found out that the only way to heaven for the children of men is through the earth" (291).[6]

Freeman's last volume of short stories, *Edgewater People* (1918), is also her poorest. Purporting to be a study of the process of growth of four villages that are the offshoot of one ancient settlement, the book is actually a loosely connected series of stories that happen to have their setting in the same area. Certain characters appear several times, but their presence in no way demonstrates Freeman's contention that communities, like individuals, inherit identical qualities from a common forebear. "I may have succeeded in making this evident in this volume," she writes in her preface. "I may have failed."[7] Unfortunately, she failed. One need not differentiate the five communities—the parent one and the four offspring—about which she writes, for they are all without any interesting characteristics, individually or together.

After 1918 Freeman published no more books and only a handful of fugitive pieces. But the 1920s held honors for her. On 23 April 1926 the American Academy of Letters awarded her the Howells Medal for distinction in fiction. The presentation was made by Hamlin Garland, an old acquaintance of hers, who characterized her work as "an unparalleled record of New England life."[8] On 10 November of the same year she was among the first four women ever to be elected to the National Institute of Arts and Letters. The other three were Agnes Repplier, Margaret Deland, and Edith Wharton. For the next four years she suffered from deteriorating health, and on 15 March 1930 she died in Metuchen. The autumn before, she had made her last visit to Randolph and Brattleboro, the places that provided her with most of what she wrote about.

Letters

In 1985 was published a volume titled *The Infant Sphinx: Collected Letters of Mary E. Wilkins Freeman,* edited with notes and biographical and critical introductions by Brent L. Kendrick. In explanation of the title of the book, Kendrick states that Henry Mills Alden, editor of *Harper's Monthly,* had nicknamed Freeman "the infant sphinx," for she "seemed so old and wise in some ways and so infantile in others."[9] The 570 letters in the collection are all that at present are known to be extant. Stylistically most of them are disappointing, for they lack the sparkle and flow of Freeman's best prose fiction. Yet they tell much about her personality, particularly the large number of them addressed to editors and publishers. Although she often, especially at the beginning of her career, deprecatingly referred to her stories as "little," she soon came to realize their worth and began to demand, though always very politely, full value for them. Reputed to be shy and unassertive socially, she was clearly not so in her business dealings. Likewise, as she became famous, she became adept and firm in warding off intruders on her time and privacy, never giving public readings or lectures and tersely refusing to comply with requests for her opinion on literary or other matters.

Personal letters, unfortunately, are not plentiful in the collection. Some of those to her editors, particularly Mary Booth, reveal a friendly relationship, as do others to her fellow writers—Jewett, Garland, Carolyn Wells among others. With a small group of friends, mostly of long standing, she carried on a more intimate correspondence. In those letters she reveals her feelings about her girlhood homes and experiences, her daily life in Randolph and Metuchen, her thoughts about marriage, and her many illnesses; and her ironic, low-keyed sense of humor—so important an ingredient in her fiction—is everywhere evident. But Freeman was not one given to laying bare her soul; her letters are those of a quite private person with a healthy sense of her own worth and the value of her accomplishment.

Reputation and Criticism to 1960

With *A Humble Romance* and *A New England Nun* Freeman established a reputation that endured throughout her life. Reviews of her work over a period of forty years were overwhelmingly favorable. Prototypical of her press notices is one in the London *Spectator* on *A New England Nun*: "The stories are among the most remarkable feats of what we may call literary impressionism in our language, so powerfully do they stamp on the reader's mind the image of the classes of individuals they portray without spending on the picture a single redundant word, a single superfluous word."[10] Holmes and Lowell and, as we have seen, Howells and Henry James were admirers of the vividness and power of her stories in the 1890s. Enhancing her transatlantic reputation was an article "Un Romancier de la Nouvelle-Angleterre," by the French author Madame Thérèse Blanc-Bentzon, in the *Revue des Deux Mondes* (August 1896).

Writing under the signature Th. Bentzon, the Frenchwoman, who was a personal friend of Jewett and who later wrote several books on America, found in Freeman *une âme* (a soul) as strange as a Russian or a Scandinavian. The French, she thought, could never fully understand *Pembroke,* for example, with its presumption of the continuing "reign" of the Bible. In Freeman, in fact, she finds lingering the spirit of seventeenth-century England—its consciousness of sin and its reference of all activities to a "spiritual end." She thinks Freeman lacks the artistic delicacy of Harriet Beecher Stowe and the imagination of Jewett, but that she enjoys a spontaneity of expression, a strong sense of realism, a poetic talent (Blanc-Bentzon cites "A Far-Away Melody"), and a painter's skill that enables her to sketch a landscape in one or two strokes. With her essay Blanc-Bentzon provides a translation into French of "A New England Nun" as an example of Freeman's skills.[11]

Freeman had long basked in her recognition by the Harper periodicals. Not only did Harper publish most of what she wrote, but the company also promoted her reputation with highly favorable editorial comments on her work. Less biased, perhaps, was the recognition conferred on her by the *Atlantic Monthly,* which in May 1899 printed one of the most profound and comprehensive analyses of her fiction ever to appear. The title of the article was "Miss Wilkins: An Idealist in Masquerade." The author, Charles Miner Thompson, traces in some detail the influence of Freeman's Puritan background on her writing with its preoccupation with abnormal volition. He draws the inevitable analogy with Hawthorne, and he correctly describes her as a pathologist of diseases of the will. In her style he sees a marked improvement between her early simplicity and the fluency beginning with *Silence*—a conclusion that few would share in. Finally, he shrewdly detects beneath her realism the Emersonian idealist who has had a vision of the mystical beneath the drab exteriors of her villagers and farmfolk.

In the same year, 1899, the *Atlantic* carried Rollin Lynde Hartt's two-piece article, "A New England Hill Town," which commended Freeman for the accuracy of her observations of society and individuals in the back country. Her reputation as a writer, a psychologist, and a social historian was now firmly established. It is not surprising, then, to find Paul Elmer More seriously comparing her with Hawthorne in an essay written for the *Independent* (July 1904) and later included in *Shelburne Essays,* second series (1905). The essay "Hawthorne: Looking Before and After" places Freeman chronologically last in a line of Puritan authors beginning with Cotton Mather and including Hawthorne as its greatest figure. Freeman, he maintains, presented the final stage of the isolating and dehumanizing tendencies in the Calvinist culture of New England—a stage of spiritual impotence and despair, but one that was ripe for an eruption back into some sort of humanism. The first sign of this reorientation to humanism he saw in *Jerome,* which he considered her best novel. The nadir of impotence, he thought, was recorded in "Two Old Lovers," which he analyzed at length.

Among academic critics Fred Lewis Pattee was the first to give Freeman serious and extensive attention, first in *A History of American Literature Since 1870* (1915) and later in "On the Terminal Moraine of New England Puritanism," a chapter in *Side-Lights on American Literature* (1922). Though he views Freeman as a realist of the Hardy, Flaubert, and Howells variety (the juxtapositions are his), Pattee otherwise sees pretty much eye to eye with Thompson, from whom he may have derived most of his ideas. To him Freeman is the anatomist of the Puritan will, the recorder of the last gasp of the old theocracy, the laureate of New England's decline.

For the next fifteen years Freeman's literary stock remained firm. In 1915 Howells used her work as a touchstone by which to assess Robert Frost's *A Boy's Will* and *North of Boston*.[12] Blanche Colton Williams in *Our Short Story Writers* (1926) devoted over twenty pages to Freeman's life, art, and methods of work; she concluded that Freeman's best stories will endure as evocations of a place and an era. John Macy in "The Passing of the Yankee," published in the *Bookman* (August 1931) shortly after Freeman's death and on the three hundredth anniversary of the founding of Boston, considered Freeman's work before 1900 among the outstanding memorials to a vanishing way of life.[13] Less general were F. O. Matthiessen's comments in an article titled "New England Stories." Among American writers, Matthiessen found Freeman "unsurpassed . . . in her ability to give the breathless intensity of a moment."[14] He also caught in her work a deep sense of the tragic dimension of life—a Melvillean awareness of the darker side of human nature: "The struggle of the heart to live by its own strength alone is her constant theme, and the sudden revolt of a spirit that will endure no more from circumstance provides her most stirring dramas."[15] He pointed out parallels between Freeman's life and works and those of Emily Brontë, Freeman's essay on whom we have already discussed.

Matthiessen's remarks echo—though very likely coincidentally— ideas expressed a generation earlier by the British critic Arthur Machen in a volume called *Hieroglyphics: A Note upon Ecstasy in Literature* (1902). Machen's thesis is that fine literature concerns itself solely with the expression of ecstasy; all else is merely reading matter, and to Machen this inferior category includes such authors as Jane Austen, George Eliot, and Thackeray. Ecstasy Machen defines as the expression of, or contact with, the *other self* (which is usually unconscious)—that is, with the spiritual, eternal, supernatural side of a human being. "There is a world elsewhere; its speech is called poetry,"[16] poetry not necessarily being metrical language. Machen classified much of Freeman's work before 1900 as literature of ecstasy, mainly because of the impression of remoteness and loneliness that pervades her pages. Loneliness "is merely another synonym for that property [ecstasy] which makes the difference between real literature and reading-matter. . . . So this is my plea for Miss Wilkins. I think that she has indicated the condition of 'ecstasis'; she has painted a society, indeed, but a society in which each man stands apart, responsible only for himself and to himself, conscious only of himself and his God. . . . This doctrine of awful, individual loneliness prevails so far that it is carried into the necessary and ordinary transactions of social life, often with results that are very absurd."[17] But to Machen the presence of absurdity in no way invalidates Freeman's work, any more than it would to an existentialist. The exercise of the individual will, in solitude, choosing its own direction and creating its possessor's very being, is the important thing—not whether the resultant action is prudent or absurd. Thus Machen insists that even Marcus Woodman's farcical sit-in on the church steps for ten years ("A Conflict Ended") serves as "a witness to the everlasting truth that, at last, each man must stand or fall alone, and that if he would stand he must, to a certain extent, live alone with his own soul"[18]—a view with overtones of Calvinism. In his lifetime Machen (1863–1947) was best known for his stories of fantasy and the supernatural. Interestingly, another British writer, Sir Arthur Conan Doyle, with similar literary concerns, also wrote, at about the same time as Machen, in high praise of Freeman, like him singling out *Pembroke* for special commendation.[19]

For approximately thirty years after her death Freeman's reputation was partly eclipsed. Most anthologies of American literature during the period (and later) contained at least one story from her pen. Often her contribution stands side by side with one by Jewett. In general the accompanying commentaries, when they engage in criticism at all, concur with the verdict given by Carlos Baker in *Literary History of the United States* (1948). Baker considers Jewett and Freeman the best artists among delineators of rural and village characters in New England. Jewett, he thinks, was able to sustain her art at a higher level, but Freeman at her best was her equal. Moreover, in the first two collections of Freeman's stories he discovers "a sharpness of line and directness of purpose . . . which even Miss Jewett could not match." In

certain of her stories he believes "there is a suggestion of hidden sub-
limations of which a Freudian might have made much."[20]

Among other cultural and literary histories to give attention, usually
quite limited, to Freeman's works were Vernon L. Parrington's *The
Beginnings of Critical Realism in America* (1930); Arthur H.Quinn's
American Fiction: A Historical Survey (1936); I. H. Herron's *The Small
Town in American Literature* (1939); and Van Wyck Brooks's *New England: Indian Summer* (1940). Of these Brooks's comments are the most
extensive, though only the early part of Freeman's career lies within
the scope of his book. To him her tales are "plain, stark, factual" tran-
scriptions of the realities of a region's decadence, worthy of comparison
with O'Neill's *Mourning Becomes Electra*—and, perhaps, *Desire Under the
Elms*: "There was something fierce and primitive in her view of life,
and the Furies existed for her. . . ." He, too, attributes to her a tragic
vision, which he thought came from "the grand inheritance of the Puritan faith; and this gave her a profundity that made her point of view,
at moments, all but universal." Like most later critics, Brooks gives
only brief attention to her novels; but of her short fiction he concludes
that "in some of her early tales, perhaps twenty or thirty, she was an
eminent artist, as eminent as Miss Jewett, and even more so, because
of the depth of feeling that informed her art."[21]

In 1951 Perry Westbrook included a chapter headed "The Anatomy
of the Will: Mary Wilkins Freeman" in his *Acres of Flint: Authors of
Rural New England, 1870–1900* (in the second edition of the book the
subtitle is *Sarah Orne Jewett and Her Contemporaries*), in which Freeman
is discussed as a major figure in a group of authors, mainly women,
that included Jewett, Rose Terry Cooke, Alice Brown, Stowe, Celia
Thaxter, and Lucy Larcom. Five years later appeared the first book
exclusively on Freeman, Edward Foster's *Mary E. Wilkins Freeman,* a
critical biography written first as a Harvard dissertation. For any one
with more than a passing interest in Freeman this book is invaluable,
and it has provided material and an impetus for a veritable spate of
writing on her. It contains numerous and substantial excerpts from her
letters, and it records reminiscences of her that Foster gleaned from her
surviving friends and neighbors in the places where she lived. It also
gives details of her relations and dealings with her editors and publishers and traces the critical reception of her works as they appeared in
print. Foster's own critical focus is on Freeman as a recorder of the
mores, customs, and attitudes—he lumps the three under the phrase

"the code"—of New England village culture; but he does not confine his critical comments solely to this aspect of Freeman's writings.

Reputation and Criticism after 1960

Owing partly, perhaps, to Foster's book, the mid-1960s saw an up-surge in interest in, and writing about, Freeman, especially among academic critics. In 1966 was published Abigail Ann Hamblen's *The New England Art of Mary E. Wilkins Freeman,* which focuses on Free-man's early stories, *Pembroke,* and *Giles Corey,* finding in them "the very essence of New England culture: strength of will, pride in the face of defeat and hopelessness, the enduring Protestant spirit with its accom-panying triumph of the individual."[22] Also in 1966 Austin Warren included a chapter on Freeman in his book *The New England Conscience*; and Larzer Ziff in his *The American 1890s* gave attention to Freeman's writing during the decade, including her novels. Ziff finds much to commend in her work but regrets that her need to make money con-flicted with her penchant for realism, as for example in *Jerome,* the naturalism of which was spoiled by a contrived happy ending. The next year, 1967, the first edition of this volume was published.

Beginning in the mid-sixties with an essay by David Hirsch in *Stud-ies in Short Fiction* (Spring 1965) titled "Subdued Meaning in 'A New England Nun,'" critics began to pay closer attention than previously to subtleties of style, imagery, and structure in Freeman's work. Hirsch undertook, with considerable success, to trace in "A New England Nun" the development of a basic tension—"a conflict between order and disorder"—by a succession of "images that become a pervasive and clearly recognizable pattern in the story."[23] To these images Hirsch attaches meanings suggested in part by the theories of Jung and Frye. A bit more down-to-earth is Joseph McElrath, Jr.'s, analysis of the structure of "The Revolt of Mother," which he finds to be a masterpiece of magazine fiction—a series of suspense-building crises with a surprise ending.[24] Like Hirsch, most recent critics of Freeman have dealt with her conscious or unconscious use of symbolism, and in the case of some stories the interpretations have been varied, as has been seen in earlier discussions on these pages. Particularly interesting have been the crit-ics' remarks on the symbolic significance of houses in Freeman's fiction. The very explicit title of Marilyn Davis DeEulis's "'Her Box of a House': Spatial Restrictions as Psychic Signpost in Mary Wilkins Free-

man's 'The Revolt of Mother'" typifies the interpretations of house
symbolism in essays by a number of other authors.[25] Thus Wood finds
that in "An Honest Soul" Martha Patch's tiny house is "no home, but
a claustrophobic trap," comparable to a coffin since Martha came close
to dying in it.[26] And Glasser finds that rooms as well as houses circum-
scribe the lives of Freeman's characters, as in "A Moral Exigency," in
which story she has also noted Freeman's Hawthornesque use of mirrors
to reveal concealed truths about a character, in this case the duality of
the heroine's personality.[27] On a somewhat broader scale Susan Toth
interprets Freeman's "The Three Old Sisters and an Old Beau" (in *The
Love of Parson Lord*) as a "parable of wasted life" or "an allegory of life
in many declining New England villages" in which run-out Puritanism
and economic and social decay are reflected in the warped or paralyzed
wills of the inhabitants. Toth rightly compares the story in theme and
method to Hawthorne's "A Wedding Knell."[28] As a final example of
symbolic interpretation in Freeman criticism, Sarah Sherman discerns
in the title character of "Christmas Jenny" (in *A New England Nun*) an
"incarnation of archaic Woman, unwedded to the specific, hence uncompromised and untainted by incorporation within the patriarchal
structure."[29]

   Sherman apparently was writing from a feminist point of view and
thus may be taken as representative of a large group of feminist critics
who have in recent years directed their attention to Freeman's writings.
A theme common to most of these critics is that Freeman is presenting,
in Marjorie Pryse's words, some "alternative paradigms for American
experience."[30] Stranded in their impoverished towns, from which so
many of the young and energetic men have fled, the women have fash-
ioned for themselves ways of life that do not depend entirely on marriage, child-raising, and taking on the age-old feminine role of
housewife in a male-dominated family. This is unquestionably the situation with many of the women in Freeman's fiction—and not only
the single women. The critics under consideration here have also
pointed out that some of Freeman's women whether married or not,
when confronted by unreasonable and dominating male demands, muster latent and, to the men, unexpected strengths and reveal an impressive spirit of independence, though some, like those in "Sister Liddy,"
are crushed totally by disease, poverty, or despair. However, women in
Freeman's world, as Michele Clark sees them, are usually "heroic. Their
demands may be small, but it is impossible to renege on them," and
she cites "A Church Mouse" and "A Mistaken Charity." She further

observes that Freeman's young women, "when forced to choose between their own economic independence or their moral integrity and a young man, . . . invariably opt for personal integrity rather than marriage."[31] Thus, as another critic has pointed out, in maintaining their independence, these women frequently had to forfeit the security and the socially sanctioned outlet for their sexuality that marriage provided.[32]

Obviously, in fashioning ways of life that deviated from the accepted norm Freeman's women were frequently in open or tacit rebellion against their communities. In an essay discussing this situation, Susan Toth writes that "in Freeman's villages, each individual must battle the community in order to define his [or her] rights and responsibilities."[33] In Toth's view the male as well as the female, the young as well as the old, villagers must struggle to win and to retain their independence, though in discussing Freeman she focuses on the struggles of women, if for no other reason than that Freeman wrote more about women than she did about men. But, as Glasser has remarked, the struggles of the women are often only temporarily successful. Having won a point, these women are likely to lapse back into subserviency, as in "A Church Mouse," "The Revolt of Mother," and "A Village Singer."

But whatever the outcome of a woman's rebellion in Freeman's writings, the feminist critics find that other women are ready to support her. As Clark and others note, this is not to say that sweetness and light reign uninterrupted among the village women. There is plenty of quarreling, backbiting, envy, and vindictiveness among them. Yet they do constitute a community of gender—much more than do the men—and more often than not they stick together and support one another. This sense of togetherness, it has been suggested, arises partly because of the women's being stranded in impoverished villages that have been abandoned by many of the men and partly because of their inferior political and economic status forced upon them by society at large. People at a disadvantage tend to band together.

Several of the critics under discussion emphasize the economic conditions that influenced life, especially that of women, in the rural New England about which Freeman wrote. Ann Douglas Wood in an essay in *Women's Studies,* "The Literature of Impoverishment: The Women Local Colorists in America, 1865–1914," does not confine herself to New England, but she finds that conditions there existed elsewhere in rural America, especially in the South. She finds, also, that the lives of the writers themselves were marked by much the same spiritual, if not material, impoverishment as were the lives of the people in their fiction. Thus these authors created a world "in diametric contrast to the lush and fecund world"[34] of the sentimental authors who flourished in the previous generation. In summary, Wood concludes that scarcity and starkness controlled the lives of the people in the local-colorists' writings. They live in bleak houses. They have lost the feminine luster that goes with homemaking and that gave them a status in sentimental fiction. Most of the women that the local-colorists write about are no longer young; few of them are mothers and thus they are deprived of the status that attaches itself to motherhood. Their creators often seem to go out of their way to make them physically unattractive if not actually deformed. Wood's essay is indeed helpful reading for an in-depth understanding of the rural lives about which Freeman and others like her (for example, her contemporary New Englander, Rose Terry Cooke) wrote.

Wood's view of rural life as depicted by the so-called local-colorists is negative as compared to that of Clark or Toth. But much more negative, indeed fiercely so, is that of Alice Brand. "Freeman's characters," she writes, "are the New England peasantry. They are the leftovers of society—the spinsters, widows and widowers, bachelors, and elderly—living civilized but neglected lives."[35] Obviously Brand is accepting in large measure the opinions of observers like Hartt regarding the decadence and demoralization of much of rural New England at the end of the nineteenth century. Unlike some of the critics just discussed, she is almost impartial in her negative opinions of both men and women in Freeman's writings. She considers the men to be ignorant, bestial, and stupid, governed only by the time-worn rules of their time and place. But the women also comport themselves by the same rules; or when they rebel against the men, "self-destructive tendencies permeate [their] aggression."[36] Men and women, if they attempt to release themselves from the "peasant" tradition in which they are trapped, do so by rage, martyrdom, submissiveness, or other self-damaging behavior—all of them frustrating in their results. In Brand's eyes most of Freeman's characters, regardless of gender, are contemptible, if not down-right hateful. She sees Freeman as depicting a way of life in which it is impossible for the sexes to live in harmony. The only remedy would be an abandonment of the traditional mores and bankrupt values in which the lives of these persons are encased. As a study of the havoc wrought by a narrow and inflexible parochialism in regard to conduct—in this case a fossilized residual Puritanism—Brand's essay is significantly more than a critique of one author's work.

Autobiographical elements in Freeman's writings have increasingly interested critics, most notably Leah Blatt Glasser, who in an essay in the *Massachusetts Review* (Summer 1984) titled "Mary E. Wilkins Freeman: The Stranger in the Mirror," has written: "A subject that haunts almost all of [Freeman's] work is the psychology of self-division of women who attempt to rebel. The conflict she struggled with throughout her life between rebellion and submission, self-fulfillment and acceptability, became the central focus of her work."[37] In support of her theme Glasser cites the case of the heroine of "A Moral Exigency," in which a dual conflict is recorded: a girl's refusal to do the conventional thing and marry, and her reluctant decision not to accept the love of her friend's fiancé, who Glasser suggests is modeled on Hanson Tyler, Freeman's lifelong but unrequited love. Speculations such as these on the relation between Freeman's inner life and the problems of her characters are supported by her own long delay in getting married—and other men than Tyler were available—while she dedicated herself to her work. In another essay, "She Is the One You Call Sister," Glasser notes that some women in Freeman's stories do "define their lives in terms of their work."[38] Moreover, marriage, even to Tyler, would have infringed on her own hard-won self-definition—or so Glasser infers. Rejection of marriage perhaps gave her a sense of power; or at least, Glasser suggests, the enigmatic unpublished fragment on Jane Lennox indicates that such may have been the case. Glasser also ponders whether "A New England Nun" may reflect Freeman's ambivalence concerning Tyler's failure to respond to her love, for had he done so she might have had to surrender that part of her selfhood that was expressed by her work. In her doctoral dissertation, "In a Closet Hidden: The Life and Work of Mary Wilkins Freeman," Glasser has traced in great detail and depth autobiographical overtones in Freeman's writings.

As critical interest in Freeman grew, her works, most of them out of print, once more became available. In 1971 *Pembroke* was published in an edition prepared by Perry Westbrook, and several reprint houses have reissued a number of her novels and many of her short-fiction collections. In addition, Michele Clark, Barbara Solomon, and Marjorie Pryse have each edited a volume of selected short stories by Freeman and provided critical introductions or afterwords. Solomon's volume also includes selections from Sarah Orne Jewett, a natural juxtaposition.

It is clear that most of the critics cited in this chapter and earlier perceive in Freeman's best work much more than "local color." Whether the special quality is called tragic vision, profundity, or ecstasy, there has been general agreement since 1890 that, though Freeman presents an ample and detailed canvas of the New England village, she also bathes her subject in tints of universality and eternity. She has succeeded in conveying a sense of the human condition—the human condition in its New England manifestations. In his *The American Scene* (1907), Henry James remarks that in New England the landscape seemed to be uttering a plea: not so much "a 'Live upon me and thrive by me' as a 'Live *with* me, somehow, and let us make out together what we may do for each other—something that is not merely estimable in more or less greasy greenbacks.'"[39] In Freeman's writing the countrymen and the countrywomen are struggling—not always unsuccessfully—to answer this plea. In New England, Jewett wrote, "the stories of strange lives have been whispered to the earth, their thoughts have burned themselves into the cold rocks."[40]

Freeman, then, may be said to be a writer who deals with universalities as revealed in a specific region. Nor is the region upon which she focuses her talents a negligible backwater in American culture. It is a region that has been seminal and transcontinentally influential in forming the American character and in establishing the national values. No major Northern author of the nineteenth century failed to realize this function of New England. Harriet Beecher Stowe's remarks in the preface to *Oldtown Folks* (1869) are only slightly colored by regional chauvinism: "New England has been to these United States what the Dorian hive was to Greece. It has always been a capital country to migrate from, and North, South, East, and West have been populated largely from New England, so that the seed-bed of New England was the seed-bed of this great American Republic, and of all that is likely to become of it."[41]

Over twenty years ago the *New Yorker* (26 March 1966) printed a sensitive extended comment on Freeman, "Item, One Empty House," by Sylvia Townsend Warner.[42] A mood piece—half story, half essay—it recounts the British author's experience as a house guest in Connecticut. Most of what she knew of New England she had read in novels and stories, especially those of Freeman. But when she mentioned Freeman to her American literary friends, she was informed that that author was no longer held in much esteem. So she kept her thoughts to herself, in the meanwhile indulging in reminiscences of

Freeman's work, for which she evidences a deeply perceptive appreciation. Awake before her hosts the morning after a party, she took a walk along the snowy country roads. Her attention was attracted by an old farmhouse tall and gaunt in the whitened meadows. Approaching closer, she noticed foot tracks a week or more old leading up to the door but none coming out. She had encountered a tale by Mary Wilkins Freeman—an unfinished tale. Unlike most Americans, then and now, Warner knew that Freeman's New England still had its home in the American psyche.

Notes and References

Chapter One

1. See Harold F. Wilson, *The Hill Country of Northern New England* (New York: Columbia University Press, 1936), for a full account of the conditions described in this chapter.

2. Fred Lewis Pattee, *Sidelights on American Literature* (New York, Century, 1922). The phrase occurs in a chapter heading.

3. Edward Foster, *Mary E. Wilkins Freeman* (New York: Hendricks House, 1956), 14.

4. Ibid., 9.

5. Brent L. Kendrick, ed., *The Infant Sphinx: Collected Letters of Mary E. Wilkins Freeman* (Metuchen, N.J.: Scarecrow Press, 1985), 372.

6. Ibid., 381.

7. Ibid., 397.

8. Ibid., 431–32.

9. Foster, *Freeman*, 51.

10. *A Humble Romance and Other Stories* (New York: Harper & Brothers, 1887), 36; hereafter cited in the text.

11. Alice Glarden Brand, "Mary Wilkins Freeman: Misanthropy as Propaganda," *New England Quarterly* 50 (March 1977):86.

12. Leah Blatt Glasser, "In a Closet Hidden: The Life and Work of Mary Wilkins Freeman" (Ph.D. diss., Brown University, 1983), 79–83.

13. Foster, *Freeman*, 53.

14. "A Maiden Lady," *Century Magazine* 30 (August 1885):654.

15. "The Old-Maid Aunt," in *The Whole Family: A Novel by Twelve Authors* (New York: Harper & Brothers, 1908), 30–59.

16. Kendrick, *Infant Sphinx*, 385.

Chapter Two

1. Kendrick, *Infant Sphinx*, 447–48.

2. *A Humble Romance and Other Stories*, Author's Edition (Edinburgh: David Douglas, 1890), v–vi.

3. Rollin Lynde Hartt, "A New England Hill Town," pt. 1, *Atlantic Monthly* 83 (April 1899):564.

4. Kendrick, *Infant Sphinx*, 224.

5. Rudyard Kipling, *Something of Myself* (New York: Doubleday, Doran, 1937), 118–19.

6. Ibid., 127.

7. Rudyard Kipling, *Times* (London), 29 November 1892, 8.

8. William Dean Howells, "The Editor's Easy Chair," *Harper's Monthly* 131 (September 1915):635.

9. Michele Clark, afterword to *The Revolt of Mother and Other Stories*, by Mary E. Wilkins Freeman (Old Westbury, N.Y.: Feminist Press, 1974), 184–85. See also Glasser, "In a Closet Hidden," 40–51, for an analysis of the social and psychological forces at work in this story.

10. Ann Douglas Wood, "The Literature of Impoverishment: The Women Local Colorists in America," *Women's Studies* 1 (1972):22.

11. Brand, "Mary Wilkins Freeman," 93.

12. Clark, afterword, 179.

13. Leah Blatt Glassner, "Mary E. Wilkins Freeman: The Stranger in the Mirror," *Massachusetts Review* 25 (Summer 1984):323–39, and "In a Closet Hidden," 177–82; Barbara Johns, "Some Reflections on the Spinster in New England Literature," in *Regionalism and the Female Imagination*, ed. Emily Toth (New York: Human Sciences Press, 1985), 33; and Clark, afterword, 188.

14. Foster, *Freeman*, 42.

15. Marjorie Pryse, afterword to *Selected Stories of Mary E. Wilkins Freeman* (New York: W. W. Norton, 1983), 318.

16. Willa Cather, introduction to *The Best Short Stories of Sarah Orne Jewett* (Boston: Houghton Mifflin, 1925), 1:xvi.

17. Blanche Colton Williams, *Our Short Story Writers* (New York: Dodd, Mead, 1926), 173.

18. "The Girl Who Wants to Write: Things to Do and Not to Do," *Harper's Bazar* 47 (June 1913):272.

19. William Dean Howells, "The Editor's Study," *Harper's New Monthly* 75 (September 1887):640.

Chapter Three

1. *A New England Nun and Other Stories* (New York: Harper & Brothers, 1891), 16–17; hereafter cited in the text.

2. Kendrick, *Infant Sphinx*, 69.

3. For comments on "A New England Nun" see Glasser, "In a Closet Hidden," 52–63; David H. Hirsch, "Subdued Meaning in 'A New England Nun,'" *Studies in Short Fiction* 2 (Spring 1965):124–36; Johns, "Some Reflections on the Spinster," 43–45; Pryse, afterword, 317–18 and "An Uncloistered 'New England Nun,'" *Studies in Short Fiction* 20 (Fall 1983):289–95; Susan Allen Toth, "The Rarest and Most and Most Peculiar Grape: Versions of the New England Woman in Nineteenth-Century Local Color," in *Regionalism*, ed. Toth, 23–24; and Wood, "Literature of Impoverishment," 21.

4. Foster, *Freeman*, 108; Glasser, "In a Closet Hidden," 52–63; Hamlin Garland, *Roadside Meetings* (New York; Macmillan, 1952), 33–34.

5. Kendrick, *Infant Sphinx*, 14.

6. Alice Hall Petry, "Freeman's New England Elegy," *Studies in Short Fiction* 21 (Winter 1984):68–70.

7. Thomas Gray, *Complete Poems,* ed. H. W. Starr and J. R. Henrickson (Oxford: Clarendon Press, 1966), 37.

8. Glasser, "In a Closet Hidden," 235.

9. Wood, "Literature of Impoverishment," 25–26.

10. Pryse, introduction to *Selected Stories of Mary E. Wilkins Freeman,* viii.

11. Kipling, *Something of Myself,* 128.

12. Glasser, "In a Closet Hidden," 137–46; Pryse, afterword, 327–29 and "The Humanity of Women in Freeman's 'A Village Singer,'" *Colby Library Quarterly* 19 (June 1983):69–77; Susan Allen Toth, "A Defiant Light: A Positive View of Mary Wilkins Freeman," *New England Quarterly* 46 (March 1973):84–87, and "The Rarest Grape," 17.

13. "An Autobiography," *Saturday Evening Post* 190 (8 December 1917):25, 75; Foster, *Freeman,* 91–92; Kendrick, *Infant Sphinx,* 39.

14. Williams, *Our Short Story Writers,* 169.

15. Kendrick, *Infant Sphinx,* 225.

16. See Anne Romines, "A Place for 'A Poetess,'" *Markham Review* 12 (Summer 1983):61–64, for an extended discussion of "A Poetess."

17. Pryse, afterword, 333.

18. Ibid., 330–31.

19. See John W. Crowley, "Freeman's Yankee Tragedy: 'Amanda and Love,'" *Markham Review* 5 (Spring 1976):58–60.

20. Susan Toth, "A Defiant Light," 83.

21. "New England in the Short Story," *Atlantic Monthly* 67 (June 1891):846.

Chapter Four

1. Kendrick, *Infant Sphinx,* 324.

2. Jonathan Edwards, *Freedom of the Will,* ed. Paul Ramsey (New Haven: Yale University Press, 1957), 258.

3. Ibid., 367.

4. Oliver Wendell Holmes, *The Autocrat of the Breakfast Table* (Boston: Houghton, Mifflin, 1889), 33.

5. Foster, *Freeman,* 52.

6. Ralph Waldo Emerson, *Essays: First Series,* ed. Joseph Slater et al. (Cambridge, Mass.: Harvard University Press, Belknap Press, 1979), 50.

7. Ralph Waldo Emerson, *The Conduct of Life* (Boston: Houghton Mifflin, 1904), 27–28.

8. Ibid., 42.

9. Ibid., 41.

10. Ibid., 42.

11. For further comments on "A Conflict Ended" see Pryse, afterword, 324–25, and Brand, "Mary Wilkins Freeman," 87–89. Pryse sees in the story an instance of a woman subduing a destructive masculine will; to Pryse the will is masculine, but woman represents the heart. Brand scorns the passivity of both Margy and Marcus.

12. Nathaniel Hawthorne, *The Scarlet Letter* (Ohio State University Press, 1962), 174.

Chapter Five

1. William Dean Howells, "The Editor's Easy Chair," *Harper's New Monthly* 85 (November 1892):961.

2. *Jane Field* (New York: Harper & Brothers, 1892), 33; hereafter cited in the text.

3. Foster, *Freeman,* 115.

4. *Pembroke* (New York: Harper & Brothers, 1894), 305–6; hereafter cited in text. See also, Foster, *Freeman,* 22.

5. Kendrick, *Infant Sphinx,* 201–5.

6. Preface to *Pembroke,* Biographical Edition (New York: Harper & Brothers, 1899), iii–vii.

7. Wood, "Literature of Impoverishment," 24.

8. Arthur Conan Doyle, "Mary E. Wilkins Freeman," *Harper's Weekly* 47 (21 November 1903):1880.

9. Edwin Arlington Robinson, *Untriangulated Stars: Letters of Edwin Arlington Robinson to Harry DeForest Smith,* ed. Denham Sutcliffe (Cambridge, Mass.: Harvard University Press, 1947), 174–75.

10. Ibid., 175.

11. Ibid.

12. Edwin Arlington Robinson, *Collected Poems* (New York: Macmillan, 1942), 5.

13. Foster, *Freeman,* 134–35.

14. *Madelon* (New York: Harper & Brothers, 1896), 115; hereafter cited in the text.

15. Harry Levin, *The Power of Blackness* (New York: Vintage Books, 1958), 87–88.

Chapter Six

1. Hamlin Garland, *Crumbling Idols* (Chicago: Stone & Kimball, 1894), chaps. 5–6.

2. Kendrick, *Infant Sphinx,* xv.

3. Ibid., 385.

4. Ibid., 25.

5. Ibid., 93.

6. Ibid., 83.

7. Ibid., 385; and Mary E. Wilkins Freeman, "The Girl Who Wants to Write: Things to Do and Avoid," *Harper's Bazar* 47 (June 1913):272.

8. Kendrick, *Infant Sphinx,* 93.

9. John Greenleaf Whittier, *Writings* (Boston: Houghton, Mifflin, 1893), 6:256.

10. Elizabeth Stuart Phelps [Ward], *Chapters from a Life* (Boston: Houghton, Mifflin, 1896), 263–65.

11. "The Girl Who Wants to Write," 272.

12. Kendrick, *Infant Sphinx,* 385.

13. Ibid., 382.

14. "Emily Brontë and *Wuthering Heights,*" in *The World's Great Women Novelists* (Philadelphia: Book Lovers' Library, 1901), 88.

15. Ibid., 89.

16. Ibid., 89–90.

Chapter Seven

1. *Jerome, A Poor Man* (New York: Harper & Brothers, 1897), 406; hereafter cited in the text.

2. Foster, *Freeman,* 154.

3. *The Portion of Labor* (New York: Harper & Brothers, 1901), 187; hereafter cited in the text.

4. Lucy Larcom, *A New England Girlhood* (Boston: Houghton, Mifflin, 1889), 9–10.

5. Lucy Larcom, *An Idyl of Work* (Boston: James R. Osgood, 1875), 119.

Chapter Eight

1. "Giles Corey, Yeoman," *Harper's New Monthly* 86 (December 1892):38.

2. Foster, *Freeman,* 152.

3. *The Heart's Highway* (New York: Doubleday, Page, 1900), 308.

4. Van Wyck Brooks, *New England: Indian Summer* (New York: E. P. Dutton, 1940), 465.

5. Foster, *Freeman,* 142–43.

6. Ibid., 143.

7. Glasser, "In a Closet Hidden," 50.

8. Clark, afterword, 186–87.

9. Wood, "Literature of Impoverishment," 27–28.

10. Ibid., 26.

11. Ibid., 27.

Chapter Nine

1. Kendrick, *Infant Sphinx,* 272–74.
2. Ibid., 274.
3. Ibid., 334.
4. Williams, *Our Short Story Writers,* 163–64.
5. Review of *The Whole Family, Nation* 87 (3 December 1908):553.
6. Susan Oaks, "The Haunting Will: The Ghost Stories of Mary E. Wilkins Freeman," *Colby Library Quarterly* 21 (December 1985):219. See also Edward Wagenknecht, introduction to *Collected Ghost Stories of Mary E. Wilkins Freeman* (Sauk City, Wis.: Arkham House, 1974), for a favorable view regarding Freeman's stories of the supernatural.
7. *Six Trees* (New York: Harper & Brothers, 1903), 79–80; hereafter cited in the text.
8. *Understudies* (New York: Harper & Brothers, 1901), 119.
9. Foster, *Freeman,* 164.
10. Brand, "Mary Wilkins Freeman," 89–90.
11. Foster, *Freeman,* 174–5.
12. Ibid., 177.
13. *The Shoulders of Atlas* (New York: Harper & Brothers, 1908), 292; hereafter cited in the text.
14. Wood, "Literature of Impoverishment," 26.
15. Kendrick, *Infant Sphinx,* 308.
16. *"Doc" Gordon* (New York: Authors and Newspapers Association, 1906), 282.
17. Kendrick, *Infant Sphinx,* 313.
18. Ibid., 312.
19. Alfred Bendixen, "It Was a Mess! How Henry James and Others Actually Wrote a Novel," *New York Times Book Review,* 27 April 1986, 3.
20. Kendrick, *Infant Sphinx,* 312.

Chapter Ten

1. *By the Light of the Soul* (New York: Harper & Brothers, 1906), 367–68; hereafter cited in the text.
2. *The Winning Lady and Others* (New York: Harper & Brothers, 1909), 42; hereafter cited in the text.
3. Kendrick, *Infant Sphinx,* 62.
4. Brand, "Mary Wilkins Freeman," 97.
5. *The Copy-Cat and Other Stories* (New York: Harper & Brothers, 1914), 64; hereafter cited in the text.
6. See Beth Wynne Fisken, "'Unusual' People in a 'Usual Place': 'The Balking of Christopher' by Mary Wilkins Freeman," *Colby Library Quarterly* 21 (June 1985):99–103, for a detailed analysis of the story, especially its Emersonian overtones.

7. *Edgewater People* (New York: Harper & Brothers, 1918), 2.

8. Foster, *Freeman,* 189.

9. Kendrick, *Infant Sphinx,* 30.

10. Quoted in Fred Lewis Pattee, *Sidelights on American Literature* (New York: Century Co. 1922), 187.

11. Th. Bentzon [Mme Thérèse Blanc-Bentzon], "Un romancier de la nouvelle-angleterre," *Revue des Deux Mondes* 136 (1 August 1896): 555–69.

12. William Dean Howells, "The Editor's Easy Chair," *Harper's Monthly* 131 (September 1915):635.

13. John Macy, "The Passing of the Yankee," *Bookman* 73 (August 1931):616–21.

14. F. O. Matthiessen, "New England Stories," in *American Writers on American Literature,* ed. John Macy (New York: Horace Liveright, 1931), 406.

15. Ibid., 408.

16. Arthur Machen, *Hieroglyphics: A Note Upon Ecstasy in Literature* (London: Unicorn Press, 1960), viii.

17. Ibid., 173–75.

18. Ibid., 176.

19. Arthur Conan Doyle, "Mary E. Wilkins Freeman," *Harper's Weekly* 47 (21 November 1903):1880.

20. Carlos Baker, "Delineation of Life and Character," in *Literary History of the United States,* ed. Robert Spiller et al. (New York: Macmillan, 1948), 2:847–48.

21. Brooks, *New England: Indian Summer,* 464–73.

22. Abigail Ann Hamblen, *The New England Art of Mary E. Wilkins Freeman* (Amherst, Mass.: Green Knight Press, 1966), 32–33.

23. Hirsch, "Subdued Meaning," 127.

24. Joseph R. McElrath, Jr., "The Artistry of Mary E. Wilkins Free-man's 'The Revolt,'" *Studies in Short Fiction* 17 (Summer 1980):255–61.

25. Marilyn Davis DeEulis, "'Her Box of a House': Spatial Restriction in Mary Wilkins Freeman's 'The Revolt of Mother,'" *Markham Review* 8 (Spring 1979):51–52.

26. Wood, "Literature of Impoverishment," 21.

27. Glasser, "Mary E. Wilkins Freeman," 327ff.

28. Susan Allen Toth, "Mary Wilkins Freeman's Parable of Wasted Life," *American Literature* 42 (January 1971):564–66.

29. Sarah W. Sherman, "The Great Goddess in New England: Mary Wilkins Freeman's 'Christmas Jenny,'" *Studies in Short Fiction* 17 (Spring 1980):157–64.

30. Marjorie Pryse, "An Uncloistered Nun," 295; see also Clark, afterword, and Susan Toth, "A Defiant Light."

31. Clark, afterword, 194–98.

32. Leah Blatt Glasser, "She Is the One You Call Sister: Discovering Mary Wilkins Freeman," in *Between Women: Biographers, Novelists, Teachers and*

Artists Write about Their Work on Women, ed. Carol Ascher et al. (Boston: Beacon Press, 1984), 190.

33. Susan Toth, "A Defiant Light," 84.

34. Wood, "Literature of Impoverishment," 16.

35. Brand, "Mary Wilkins Freeman," 83.

36. Ibid., 84.

37. Glasser, "Mary E. Wilkins Freeman," 323.

38. Glasser, "She Is the One," 189–93.

39. Henry James, *The American Scene* (New York: Harper & Brothers, 1907), 20.

40. Sarah Orne Jewett, *A White Heron and Other Stories* (Boston: Houghton, Mifflin, 1886), 25.

41. Harriet Beecher Stowe, *Oldtown Folks* (Boston: Fields, Osgood, 1869), iii.

42. Sylvia Townsend Warner, "Item, One Empty House," *New Yorker* 42 (26 March 1966):131–38.

Selected Bibliography

PRIMARY SOURCES

1. Short Fiction
The Copy-Cat and Other Stories. New York: Harper & Brothers, 1914.
Edgewater People. New York: Harper & Brothers, 1918.
The Fair Lavinia and Others. New York: Harper & Brothers, 1907.
The Givers. New York: Harper & Brothers, 1904.
A Humble Romance and Other Stories. New York: Harper & Brothers, 1887.
The Love of Parson Lord and Other Stories. New York: Harper & Brothers, 1900.
A New England Nun and Other Stories. New York: Harper & Brothers, 1891.
The People of Our Neighborhood. Philadelphia: Curtis Publishing Co., 1898.
Silence and Other Stories. New York: Harper & Brothers, 1898.
Six Trees. New York: Harper & Brothers, 1903.
Understudies. New York: Harper & Brothers, 1901.
The Wind in the Rose-Bush and Other Stories of the Supernatural. New York: Doubleday, Page, 1903.
The Winning Lady and Others. New York: Harper & Brothers, 1909.

2. Collections of Short Fiction
The Best Stories of Mary E. Wilkins. Introduction by H. W. Lanier. New York: Harper & Brothers, 1927.
The Revolt of Mother and Other Stories. Edited with afterword by Michele Clark. Old Westbury, N.Y.: Feminist Press, 1974.
Selected Stories of Mary E. Wilkins Freeman. Edited with introduction and afterword by Marjorie Pryse. New York: W. W. Norton, 1983.
Short Fiction of Sarah Orne Jewett and Mary Wilkins Freeman. Edited with introduction by Barbara H. Solomon. New York: New American Library, 1979.

3. Novels
An Alabaster Box. New York: D. Appleton & Co., 1917. With Florence Morse Kingsley.
The Butterfly House. New York: Dodd, Mead, 1912.
By the Light of the Soul. New York: Harper & Brothers, 1906.
The Debtor. New York: Harper & Brothers, 1905.
"Doc" Gordon. New York: Authors and Newspapers Association, 1906.
Evelina's Garden. New York: Harper & Brothers, 1899.

The Heart's Highway, A Romance of Virginia. New York: Doubleday, Page, 1900.
The Jamesons. New York: Doubleday & McClure, 1899.
Jane Field. New York: Harper & Brothers, 1893.
Jerome, A Poor Man. New York: Harper & Brothers, 1897.
Madelon. New York: Harper & Brothers, 1896.
Pembroke. New York: Harper & Brothers, 1894. Reprint. Edited with introduction by Perry D. Westbrook. New Haven, Conn.: College and University Press, 1971.
The Portion of Labor. New York: Harper & Brothers, 1901.
The Shoulders of Atlas. New York: Harper & Brothers, 1908.
The Whole Family: A Novel by Twelve Authors. New York: Harper & Brothers, 1908. By Mary Wilkins Freeman, William Dean Howells, Henry James et al.
The Yates Pride: A Romance. New York: Harper & Brothers, 1912.

4. Drama
Giles Corey, Yeoman: A Play. New York: Harper & Brothers, 1893.

5. Poetry
"Boy's Love." Century 26 (October 1883):959.
"It Was a Lass." Century 27 (April 1884):959.
"A Maiden Lady." Century 30 (August 1885):654.
"Sweet Phyllis." Century 24 (September 1882):799.

6. Writings for Children
The Adventures of Anne: Stories of Colonial Times. Boston: D. Lothrop, [1886].
Comfort Pease and Her Gold Ring. New York: Fleming H. Revell, 1895.
The Cow with the Golden Horns and Other Stories. Boston: D. Lothrop, [1884].
Decorative Plaques. Designs by George F. Barnes. Poems by Mary E. Wilkins. Boston: D. Lothrop, [1883].
The Green Door. New York: Moffat Yard, 1910.
Once Upon a Time and Other Child-Verses. Boston: Lothrop Publishing Company, [1897].
The Pot of Gold and Other Stories. Boston: D. Lothrop, [1892].
Young Lucretia and Other Stories. New York: Harper & Brothers, 1892.

7. Selected Miscellaneous and Uncollected Prose
"An Autobiography," Saturday Evening Post 190 (8 December 1917):25, 75. Not an autobiography but a discussion of "The Revolt of Mother."
"Mary E. Wilkins Freeman." In My Maiden Effort: Being Personal Confessions of Well-Known American Authors as to Their Literary Beginnings, 265–67. Garden City, N.Y.: Doubleday, Page, 1921. Introduction by G. Burgess.
"Emily Brontë and Wuthering Heights." In The World's Great Women Novelists,

87–93. Philadelphia: Book Lovers' Library, [1901].
"The Girl Who Wants to Write: Things To Do and Avoid." *Harper's Bazar* 47 (June 1913):272.
"Good Wits, Pen and Paper." In *What Women Can Earn,* by G. H. Dodge et al., 28–29. New York: Frederick A. Stokes, 1899.
"The Long Arm." In *The Long Arm and Other Detective Stories,* 1–66. London: Chapman & Hall, 1895. With J. Edgar Chamberlain.
"Pastels in Prose." *Harper's New Monthly* 86 (December 1892):147–48.
"Wake Up America!" In *America in the War,* edited by Louis Raemakers, 34. New York: Century, 1918.
"We Are for France." In *For France,* edited by Charles H. Towne, 336. Garden City, N.Y.: Doubleday, Page, 1917.

8. Published Letters
The Infant Sphinx: Collected Letters of Mary E. Wilkins Freeman. Edited with introduction and annotations by Brent L. Kendrick. Metuchen, N.J.: Scarecrow Press, 1985.

SECONDARY SOURCES

1. Bibliographies
Blanck, J. N. "Mary E. Wilkins Freeman." In *Bibliography of American Literature.* Vol. 3. New Haven: Yale University Press, 1959, 324–43. Contains only items published as books or parts of books.
Kendrick, Brent L. "Mary E. Wilkins Freeman." *American Literary Realism* 8 (Summer 1975):255–57. Lists and discusses briefly twelve dissertations written before 1975 and dealing wholly or in part with Freeman.

2. Books
Foster, Edward. *Mary E. Wilkins Freeman.* New York: Hendricks House, 1956. The only book-length biography. Excellent coverage of Freeman's life and background; contains much critical comment and the most nearly complete bibliographies available. Pages 210–22 contain the most nearly complete listing thus far of Freeman's books, articles, and uncollected articles, stories, and poems, and of articles about her before 1951. Individual stories in each one of her collections of stories are named.
Hamblen, Abigail Ann. *The New England Art of Mary E. Wilkins Freeman.* Amherst, Mass.: Green Knight Press, 1966. Finds in Freeman's works "the very essence of New England culture: strength of will, pride in the face of defeat and hopelessness, the enduring Protestant spirit with its accompanying triumph of the individual." Focus is on the early stories, *Pembroke,* and *Giles Corey.*

3. Parts of Books

Brooks, Van Wyck. *New England: Indian Summer.* New York: E. P. Dutton, 1940, 464–73. General comment on Freeman as a depictor of economic and spiritual decline in New England.

Herron, Ima. *The Small Town in American Literature.* Dallas: Southern Methodist University Press, 1969, 20–24. Discusses Freeman as an exposer of meanness of village life; emphasis on *Giles Corey.*

Howells, William Dean. *Heroines of Fiction.* 2 vols. New York: Harper & Brothers, 1901, 2:253–59. Discusses *Jane Field* and its heroine.

Johns, Barbara. "Some Reflections on the Spinster in New England Literature." In *Regionalism and the Female Imagination,* edited by Emily Toth, 29–64. New York: Human Sciences Press, 1985. Finds that for Freeman's spinsters their spinsterhood is "an act of moral heroism."

Machen, Arthur. *Hieroglyphics.* 1902. Reprint. London: Unicorn Press, 1960, 173–76. Highly laudatory of Freeman's work, which Machen classifies as *real* literature, that is, literature of ecstasy.

Matthiessen, F. O. "New England Stories." In *American Writers on American Literature,* edited by John Macy, 399–413. New York: Horace Liveright, 1931. Comments on Freeman's techniques and on her significance.

More, Paul Elmer. "Hawthorne: Looking Before and After." In *The Shelburne Essays.* 2d ser. Boston: Houghton Mifflin, 1905, 173–87. Places Freeman among Puritan authors from the Mathers to her own day.

Parrington, Vernon L. *The Beginnings of Critical Realism in America.* New York: Harcourt Brace, 1930, 60–69. Compares the writers of rural New England with those of the cities, finding the latter to be less realistic and more enslaved to the genteel tradition. He also attempts a correlation, though inadequate, between Freeman's *Pembroke* and Sherwood Anderson's *Wineburg, Ohio.*

Pattee, Fred Lewis. *A History of American Literature Since 1870.* New York: Century, 1915, 235–40. Places Freeman in context of her times in New England and in the nation.

————. *Sidelights on American Literature.* New York: Century, 1915. The chapter "On the Terminal Moraine of New England Puritanism" (175–209) is an account and criticism of Freeman and her works before 1920; the emphasis is on Freeman's fiction as a statement of an expiring outlook and tradition.

Quinn, Arthur H. *American Fiction: A Historical Survey.* New York: D. Appleton Century, 1936, 433–41. Brief account of Freeman's publications, their realism, and their place in American literature.

Robinson, Edwin Arlington. *Untriangulated Stars: Letters of Edwin Arlington Robinson to Harry DeForest Smith.* Edited Denham Sutcliffe. Cambridge, Mass.: Harvard University Press, 1947, 174–75. Provocative comment by a sensitive New England villager who had read *Pembroke* shortly after its publication.

Toth, Susan Allen. "'The Rarest and Most Peculiar Grape': Versions of the New England Woman in Nineteenth-Century Local Color Literature." In *Regionalism and the Female Imagination: A Collection of Essays,* edited by Emily Toth, 15–28. New York: Human Sciences Press, 1985. Sees Freeman as specializing "in portraits of neurotic women," but writing about alternatives to marriage and such subjects as mother-daughter love.

Warren, Austin. *The New England Conscience.* Ann Arbor: University of Michigan Press, 1966, 157–69. Freeman in relation to writers from William Bradford to John Marquand.

Westbrook, Perry D. *Acres of Flint: Sarah Orne Jewett and Her Contemporaries.* Rev. ed. Metuchen, N.J.: Scarecrow Press, 1981, 86–104. Discusses Freeman as one of a group of New England authors, including Jewett, Stowe, Rose Terry Cooke, and Celia Thaxter.

Williams, Blanche C. *Our Short Story Writers.* New York: Dodd, Mead, 1926, 160–81. The types of stories that Freeman wrote, their themes, their settings, their characters; information on Freeman's writing habits.

Wilson, Harold F. *The Hill Country of Northern New England.* New York: Columbia University Press, 1936. Contains valuable source material on social and economic conditions in Freeman's New England.

Ziff, Larzar. *The American 1890s.* New York: Viking Press, 1966, 192–96. Comments on the naturalism of Freeman's depiction of New England village life but deplores her lapse into sentimentalism in an effort to please public taste.

4. Articles

Bentzon, Th. [Mme Thérèse Blanc-Bentzon]. "Un romancier de la nouvelle-angleterre." *Revue des Deux Mondes* 136 (1 August 1896):544–69. Contains a French translation of "A New England Nun" and comments on Freeman as an interpreter of a Calvinist culture.

Brand, Alice Glarden. "Mary Wilkins Freeman: Misanthropy as Propaganda." *New England Quarterly* 50 (March 1977):83–100. "Freeman's characters are the New England peasantry," in the clutches of a tradition that they combat, if at all, by rage, martyrdom, and subservience.

Crowley, John W. "Freeman's Yankee Tragedy: 'Amanda and Love.'" *Markham Review* 5 (Spring 1976):58–60. Argues plausibly that Amanda and other Freeman characters achieve significant moral victories over their selfish impulses.

DeEulis, Marilyn Davis. "Her Box of a House: Spatial Restriction as Psychic Signpost in Mary Wilkins Freeman's 'The Revolt of Mother.'" *Markham Review* 8 (Spring 1979):51–52. An interesting interpretation of "The Revolt of Mother" and one that is relevant to other stories by Freeman.

Fisken, Beth Wynne. "'Unusual' People in a 'Usual Place': 'The Balking of Christopher' by Mary Wilkins Freeman." *Colby Library Quarterly* 21 (June

1985):99–103. Interprets the story in light of Freeman's transcendentalist leanings.

Glasser, Leah Blatt. "Mary E. Wilkins Freeman: The Stranger in the Mirror." *Massachusetts Review* 25 (Summer 1984):323–39. Discusses "self-division in women who attempt to rebel" in Freeman's fiction.

Hartt, Rollin Lynde. "A New England Hill Town." *Atlantic Monthly* 83 (April 1899):561–74; (May 1899):712–20. A study of cultural decay in rural New England.

Hirsch, David H. "Subdued Meaning In 'A New England Nun.'" *Studies in Short Fiction* 2 (Spring 1965):124–36. Penetrating analysis of the symbolism in "A New England Nun," with many references to Jung and Frye.

Howells, William Dean. "The Editor's Study." *Harper's New Monthly* 75 (September 1887):640. Early recognition of Freeman as an important New American writer.

Levy, Babette May. "Mutations in New England Local Color." *New England Quarterly* 19 (Summer 1946):338–58. Places Freeman in context of New England local-color writing.

Macy, John. "The Passing of the Yankee." *Bookman* 73 (August 1931):616–21. Written shortly after Freeman's death and in commemoration of the three hundreth anniversary of the founding of Boston, this article discusses the role of Freeman and others as historians of a culture that is almost extinct.

"New England in the Short Story." *Atlantic Monthly* 67 (June 1891):845–50. Unsigned article that reviews *A New England Nun* along with recently published volumes by Jewett and Annie Trumbull Slosson. Its analyses of these authors' methods and purposes are perceptive and profound. This is a germinal essay in the study of New England regionalism.

Oaks, Susan. "The Haunting Will: The Ghost Stories of Mary Wilkins Freeman." *Colby Library Quarterly* 21 (December 1985):208–20. "Freeman attributes her ghosts to the evil potential of the individual will."

Petry, Alice Hall. "Freeman's New England Elegy." *Studies in Short Fiction* 21 (Winter 1984):68–70. Echoes of Gray's "Elegy Written in a Country Churchyard" in "A New England Nun."

Pryse, Marjorie. "The Humanity of Women in Freeman's 'A Village Singer,'" *Colby Library Quarterly* 19 (June 1983):69–77. "'A Village Singer' demonstrates that a society which negates the humanity of women actually limits its potential for spiritual vision."

———. "An Uncloistered 'New England Nun.'" *Studies in Short Fiction* 20 (Fall 1983):289–95. Argues that Louisa Ellis has found a satisfactory alternate way of life to the traditional one of marriage.

Quina, James H., Jr. "Character Types in the Fiction of Mary Wilkins Freeman." *Colby Library Quarterly* 9 (June 1971):432–39. Divides Freeman's characters into four groups: maintainers of the status quo, rebels, ascetics, and moderators.

Romines, Ann. "A Place for 'A Poetess.'" *Markham Review* 12 (Summer 1983):61–64. "'A Poetess' is a valuable story because of the skill and subtlety with which Mary Wilkins Freeman considers the situation of a woman determined to live or die as an artist."

Sherman, Sarah W. "The Great Goddess in New England: Mary Wilkins Freeman's 'Christmas Jenny.'" *Studies in Short Fiction* 17 (Spring 1980):157–64. Sees in Christmas Jenny "the incarnation of archaic woman, unwedded to the specific, hence uncompromised and untainted by incorporation within the patriarchal structure."

Thompson, Charles M. "Miss Wilkins: An Idealist in Masquerade." *Atlantic Monthly* 83 (May 1899):665–75. A consideration of Freeman's themes, which Thompson finds usually to be some aspect of the Puritan will, and of her style, which he praises for concreteness and simplicity.

Toth, Susan Allen. "Defiant Light: A Positive View of Mary Wilkins Freeman." *New England Quarterly* 46 (March 1973):82–93. Finds that Freeman puts "emphasis on the positive drive towards fulfillment that motivates her strong characters, a fulfillment of what they believe to be their own true selves" despite social pressures.

———. "Mary Wilkins Freeman's Parable of Wasted Life." *American Literature* 42 (January 1971):464–67. Finds in the story "The Three Old Sisters and the Old Beau" the presence of many of Freeman's "favorite themes" and some echoes of Hawthorne's "The Wedding Knell."

Wood, Ann Douglas. "The Literature of Impoverishment: The Women Local Colorists in America 1865–1914." *Women's Studies* 1 (1972):3–40. The local-color writers, including Freeman, "actually valued, as the sentimentalists ostensibly did, the conventional feminine virtues, but they had lost faith in their potency."

5. Dissertations

Glasser, Leah Blatt. "In a Closet Hidden: The Life and Work of Mary Wilkins Freeman." Ph.D. dissertation, Brown University, 1982. Explores autobiographical elements in Freeman's fiction.

Index

WORKS — DRAMA

WORKS — NON-FICTION

WORKS — POETRY